TRAINING GAMES
COACHING RUNNERS CREATIVELY

2nd edition

Eric Anderson

Illustrations by George Anderson

TAFNEWS PRESS

Book Division of Track & Field News

First published in 1996 by Tafnews Press,
Book Division of Track & Field News,
2570 El Camino Real, Suite 606,
Mountain View, CA 94040 USA.

First edition printed in 1994.
Second edition printed in 1996.
Second printing of second edition, 1999.
Third printing of second edition, 2003.

Standard Book Number: 0-911521-47-X

Printed in the United States of America

Cover design and production: Teresa Tam

Acknowledgments

Every coach can develop his own coaching style and theoretical base from three differing modalities. First, he can be formally educated in college and can study the sport via books, magazines, and journals. Second, he applies this knowledge to the athletes he coaches and evaluates the outcome, thus gaining experience. Finally, he can observe other coaches.

Access to the first two methods is not so difficult; almost anybody can be schooled, read a dozen books, and volunteer as an assistant coach. But if a young coach can find a mentor who has done all of these and has coached a full career, he is truly fortunate. I have been this fortunate. I am thankful to my mentor Coach Paul Wood under whom I studied for 12 years. This book is designed around one of the main principles Coach Wood taught me—a little variety goes a long way.

I would also like to acknowledge all of my runners, past and present. They have supported me in my endeavors, tolerated my using them occasionally in my own researches and studies, and in many direct ways have helped develop the ideas and games described in this book.

Finally, I would like to thank Tafnews Press for asking me to write this book—particularly publisher Ed Fox who realized that there has never been an extensive compilation of training games and motivational ideas for coaching runners in print and asked me to fill the gap.

—Eric Anderson, February 1994

Contents

Introduction

Coaching distance runners is both a science and an art. Unfortunately, many coaches only concern themselves with the science of coaching. This is not hard to do, as there are plenty of books and periodicals dealing with the scientific aspects of coaching. This kind of knowledge of course is required if we are to develop competitive athletes. However, the extent to which a runner derives benefit from his training is dependent not only on the workouts the coach assigns, but the enthusiasm that the runner has for them. A well-crafted interval workout is of little value if the athlete's level of motivation is insufficient to do it with effort. This is where the art of coaching comes into play.

While the art of distance coaching is concerned with implementing workouts that accord with sound physiological principles of training at the proper time, it is also concerned with the psychological impact those workouts have on the runner. The wise coach cares about the mental state of each athlete, the entire team, and how the individual athlete interacts with the team. Artful coaching involves knowing how to motivate athletes, and teams.

It is the art of coaching, therefore, that this book addresses. It deals with maintaining motivation, increasing team cohesion, and enhancing performance. The following pages contain workouts that will bring life back into a runner's training, tactics that will enable him to race better, and motivational techniques a coach can employ to increase his runners' level of motivation. There are enough workouts and suggested variations to enable a coach to employ a unique workout almost every day.

While reading you will conjure up unique workout ideas yourself, and I encourage you to write them down. (Send us your ideas and we'll include the best ones in the next edition of this book. Send to Publisher, Tafnews Press, 2570 El Camino real, Suite 606, Mountain View, CA 94040 USA.)

The runner without a coach will also find this book immensely helpful. It will give him inspiration to create diverting ways of training and things to do while running; it will help him chase away the runner's blues and increase enjoyment in the sport. Hopefully, it will make the daily training program something to look forward to.

So whether you are a coach or a runner, we hope you'll find this book helps you enjoy what you do. Free your mind of the humdrum and the traditional. Express some freedom and creativity. Ultimately you will run better because of it, for a little variety and diversion go a long way.

Chapter 1

What Is Motivation?

It has been argued that motivation is a quality of an individual that cannot be enhanced by another; this book aims to prove that wrong. The distance coach has available to him an array of techniques and workouts that can significantly increase at least the temporary motivational state of his athletes. It is my premise that by working on short-term motivation repeatedly the coach can also increase the long-term motivation of his athletes.

Motivation can serve to improve performance in two major ways. The first is that if an athlete enjoys what he is doing he will tend to be more tenacious in his pursuits— which ultimately leads to heightened performances. Secondly, performance has been described as being a product of drive times habit strength. If drive is either wholly or in part made up of motivation, then motivation plays a key role in determining an individual's or team's level of performance.

What specifically motivates athletic endeavors? That depends on the individual athlete. The underlying premise is that the athlete has to have some needs met. There are of course, many needs the athlete may have, from simple fun to love. The workouts in this book are designed to meet the athletes needs for fun, socialization, self-expression, recognition and feelings of belonging. The coaching ideas presented are designed for these reasons and to promote, praise, and show affection for the athletes. There are also coaching suggestions which help foster a strong relationship between the coach and the athlete. The better the coach knows and understands an athletes' needs the better he will be able to help meet them.

Many of the suggestions in this book are geared toward increasing the team's cohesiveness, which leads to positive practice sessions, less absenteeism, and a sense of collective efficacy in which the team feels powerful, as a whole.

Finally, at the very least the workouts, techniques, and suggestions herein will help to ward off the runner's blues or boredom. Routine kills. There are enough workouts in this book to help keep training fun, challenging, and best of all fresh year-round. With a little imagination you can adapt many of these workouts to a variety of situations . . . or invent your own.

Chapter 2

Motivational Training Runs and Games

This chapter is devoted to making runs fun. Make runs fun? "Running can't be fun." "How can running be fun?" These are examples of common attitudes. Unfortunately, running has been used as punishment by naively punitive physical education teachers and coaches. The concept of "taking a lap" has taught society that running is something to be avoided rather than embraced. Do you think school children in Kenya think it punishment to run to school? When something is used on an individual as punishment it quickly grows unenjoyable. Using running as punishment makes about as much sense as using reading for punishment.

Truth be told, the act of running is inherently fun. Simply watch children play. What often comprises a large part of their play? Running. Running is part of most all other "enjoyable" physical activities. Why? Without delving too deeply into philosophy—running is a basic way to express our individual freedom.

Runners should make the decision to esteem running as something they do to reward themselves. Rather than saying, "I'm running to lose weight," view running as "your" time. Rank it high in developing your daily schedule. When you do something well, or endure something difficult, reward yourself with a run. This in itself is the most valuable asset toward truly enjoying the art of running.

Yet, even with such a positive mind set, I'll admit it, sometimes running can grow dull. All fun things can if you repeat them too often, especially if there is nothing new; it's always the same. In the sport of running with so many miles required for improvement, nothing new equals the runner's blues. Coaches are particularly guilty of falling into the habit of assigning the same workouts, in the same location, on the same day.

This need not be so. With a little variety we can maintain our enthusiasm and find new challenges to enjoy. There are a few training *rules*, if you will, to help maintain the enjoyment of running.

The first rule for enhancing training motivation is the rule of numbers. The more who run, the more the fun. Though there are advantages to solo jaunts, as far as runs being fun, it occurs more readily in numbers. This is chiefly due to conversation, jokes, repartee. Just as we enjoy a conversation over dinner or on a drive, we enjoy conversation during a run.

The second rule is the rule of exploration. To boldly go where no runner has gone before. Exploring new terrain, or a new city, always proves enjoyable. Perhaps the scenery of unexplored countryside, or the thrill of running through a city for the first time. If you try, you might even be able to find new areas of "your old stomping grounds" that you have not yet fully explored.

The third rule is that of dirt. The more dirt the better. Get rough, get dirty. Be brave and run through the hills, fields, ditches and mud. It's nothing a shower can't fix. I like to say that the difference between the runner and the jogger is in the cleanliness of his shoes.

If, after following these suggestions, you still can't seem to shake the blues, become creative in your workout designs. Dare to imagine. Develop creative workouts, or daydream adventures and fantasies. Break the chains that bind you to the same route, the same pace, the same time—just go.

For coaches, the most difficult job is trying to maintain the motivation of their athletes from one workout to the next. In general, we are a nation of dull coaches. Distance on Monday, speed on Wednesday, and race on Saturday. . . the same workouts season after season. Many coaches have never heard of training games, and fewer still utilize them. However, there are some creative and successful coaches who do, many of whom have contributed to this book.

Young runners, high school age in particular, tend to be creative, thrill-seeking, and open to new training ideas. But all runners—of all ages—can benefit from variety and creativity. Often runners make runs fun spontaneously, especially teams.

The cross country team I coach at Huntington Beach HS has come up with spontaneous activities during the middle of runs that have not only entertained me, but have made me laugh so hard I could no longer run. For example, one day I was trailing my sophomore team, and when I caught them, one of them said, "Look, coach, we have been practicing." I had no idea what they were talking about since we were just on a slow distance run. They proceeded to do drill team style maneuvers. Holding their hands above their heads, they lined up single file, and peeled off into different formations—sort of a drill team distance squad. The sad thing was they were pretty good, too. The coach should be careful not to squash this creativity and should in fact promote it by being a little crazy himself.

Perhaps spontaneous fun is best, but you can purposely add games to training to make them more fun or to take some of the pressure off before an important race or simply to break up the monotony of routine runs. This chapter is devoted to finding ways to making training fun, inspiring, or sometimes just plain silly. Most of the workouts require a team or group to perform, but with a little imagination . . .

I. Actual Training Games Workouts

Goofy Relays

Goofy relays are just what they sound like—goofy! The goofier the better. When I first began coaching I tried to make some of the workouts more fun by inventing relays; I thought they would be fun. The mistake I made was in saying that they were going to be fun. The runners, like high schoolers in general, were eager to prove me wrong. They complained, "This is goofx!" I used to fight them, "No, it's not!" They won.

So I gave in—and named my relays goofy relays. Now I have already admitted that they are goofy before the runners get the opportunity to do so. I make them as silly as possible. First, I may divide the team into separate teams, boys vs. girls, or by grade level, whatever. Next, I explain the first relay. I either give points per relays, or I combine all the relays into a massive, win-or-lose relay. Here are some of the possibilities:

1. Find the person with the biggest size shoe on each team and take his shoes. Each member of each team must run to a fence and back with those big shoes on. The shoes must remain on the feet. Maybe this isn't so bad for a size 10 in a size 12 shoe, but when one of the girls puts her size 5 into it, it's hilarious.

2. Have a designated pullover sweat-top, on each team, and have the runners run to a fence and back, take the sweat-top off and put it on the next person. This also allows teamwork, as teams devise the fastest way to remove and place a sweat-top over the next runner.

3. They run around a park and touch each park bench, or each tree, or whatever. They can go in any order they wish.

4. They run to a play set and: swing 10 times, go up and down the slide three times, climb up the slide and slide down backward, or otherwise utilize whatever type of play set the park may have.

5. They run a set distance, do 10 somersaults, run some more, do more somersaults, etc. . .

6. They hold water in their mouth, sprint to a fence and back, keeping the water in their mouth, not spitting it out on the coach.

7. They run backwards, or sideways.

8. Three-legged relays, tying legs together with a shirt or jacket.

9. I assign point values for objects and give the runners a certain amount of time to recover as many points worth of objects as they can. Examples: benches are worth 100, trash cans 50, cones 10, personal objects like glasses, jackets, etc. . .10. It then becomes a race, and a war.

10. You can also have them take off shoes, shirts, and hats and hide them or spread them out in a big field. Assigning point values to an article of clothing, a hat is worth five points, sunglasses are worth 10. Have two teams search for these items, the team with the most points winning.

Value: Goofy Relays aren't really intended to improve the runners' physical conditioning. They are, however, good tension breakers and help build team morale and cohesiveness.

Arm Intervals

Our arms, in anaerobic running, often grow fatigued, leading to a slower arm drive. A slower arm drive directly results in a slower leg turnover rate, resulting in slower running. To learn to deal with this fatigue, should it occur, I have developed a workout which I call Arm Intervals.

An arm interval workout is basically an anaerobic fartlek session, with pushups in the middle. The purpose of the pushups is to fatigue the arms. Under normal training circumstances your arms do not grow fatigued. Therefore, the pushups simulate race fatigue nicely. This workout must be done on grass, as follows:

After an adequate warmup, run anaerobic bursts of speed, (the exact distance or time is not important), then slowly stop, drop and do a number of pushups until your arms feel fatigued. It is not necessary to do the pushups until you reach your limit, but you do want a good deal of fatigue. Then hop back up and continue with the fast-paced running. Take a recovery, jog for an equal amount of time as the bursts of speed, then do the same again. It is helpful to have the coach yell "Run, drop, and jog" commands to the athletes.

Another variety of this workout is to have short races that include pushups. I often have my runners do relay races of 200-400 meters with four sets of 10 pushups during the run. This actually makes for some exciting workouts with great slides and all. Yet another extremely difficult workout is to run hard for a distance of one to two miles nonstop with 10 pushups every quarter-mile. This workout proves to be quite challenging and probably should be used sparingly and not in the early phases of the conditioning period.

It is crucial to work on proper form. As the main driving muscles in the arms grow fatigued, the smaller muscles are called upon to continue the effort. This often results in a loss of form.

Value: Arm intervals can be adapted to benefit the runner during any phase of the season, though they best fit during the strength or speed phases. They can be used for a middle-to hard-effort day. This workout also provides an excellent opportunity to work on upper body form during times of distress.

The Triangle

This workout was suggested to me by Rich Medellin of Esperanza High School in Southern California; it can serve as a light speed-to-strength run depending on the parameters of the game. "For this game we map out a triangle in which each leg is about 200 meters. Each team must run to the corner of the triangle and do 10 pushups. They then run to the second corner of the triangle and do 10 situps, and then to the third corner and do 10 burpees or jumping jacks."

You can do as many circuits as you want, and you can make the distance of the runs as far as you want. Coach Medellin has his runners do 10 circuits. "We start getting to the seventh lap, and they have done 70 pushups, 70 situps, and 70 burpees, and it begins to hurt. It works well on the baseball field. We go from foul pole to foul pole and then to home plate. The foul poles are 200 meters, then the next leg is relatively short. Since the whole team has to do it there is a team concept to it."

Value: The triangle is a vehicle for doing intervals. Depending on the length of the circuit you set up, this exercise serves well in the strength or speed phase of the season. It can also function as a moderate- to difficult-level workout.

Water Balloon Relays

Much like the goofy relays, water balloon relays provide for a good, easy speed session, with a few surprises. Divide the team into two groups and have relays, with or without the balloons. Assign a balloon value for each relay.

All of the goofy relays are good examples of relays that can be employed, or try these:

1. Partners must run single file; the runner in front throws the balloon over his head, and the runner behind must catch it. After he catches it, he runs to the front and tosses it over his head. If the balloon is dropped, they lose.

2. Set out water balloons throughout a park, and have them scramble for them. Much like an Easter egg hunt. Just to tick a few off, maybe blow some up with air.

3. Have them run with a big, sloshy balloon, and use it as the baton. This is a baton you can't pick up if dropped.

Once the relays are over, each team will have a number of balloons. I then take both teams and put them on opposite ends of the football field. I put a bucket of balloons at the 50-yard line, and buckets at each 40-yard line. The "war" begins at the dropping of a water balloon. This war actually involves some strategy, the team can choose to sprint to the balloons at the 50-yard line to increase their ammunition supplies, or they can take what they have, sprint to the 40-yard line, and bomb the other team attempting to recover the balloons at the 50-yard line.

For some reason, this workout always turns into a chase-the-coach-around-the-park-school-and-parking-lot-with-a-water-balloon workout. The coach is advised to keep a few extra in his car, for a little pay-back at the end of the workout. One time, I chased a runner all over the parking lot, with an empty water balloon. I thought I had him going until someone yelled to him that there was no water in it, and he began chasing me with his water balloon. After I tired, and decided to give into the splatting, he laughed. He had no water in his balloon either.

Last piece of advice, never tell your runners the day before that they are going to have water balloon relays. They sometimes come prepared with an arsenal of their own supplies.

Value: Water balloon relays are a fun/easy day's workout, though they can be modified to a moderate level of difficulty. I recommend using them during the base phase of the season to break up the monotony of distance running.

Wimps And Studs

When the coach wants a high-quality workout, without the runners knowing it in advance, he can play a game I designed called wimps and studs. After an adequate warmup, the coach simply tells the runners to do "X" amount of quick accelerations or relays. He makes them do enough to where they begin to tire, then the game begins.

The coach then says, "OK, wimps go home and studs stay." They will look perplexed. When they ask what you mean, simply repeat, "Wimps go home and studs stay." Since nobody wants to be called a wimp, they will (usually) all stay. The coach then says, "OK, studs run from here to there "X" amount of times." After they complete this, the coach says, "OK, wimps go home, studs stay." You get the idea. So will they. After a while it will turn into a competition amongst themselves to see who can last the longest. Or perhaps they will use teamwork and decide to all go home at the same time. Either way the coach wins. Just make sure nobody thinks you are really calling him or her a wimp. It is for fun only.

Value: Depending on the distances run and the length of the intervals the coach designs, this workout can fit any phase of the training pyramid. The benefit of the workout will wear off if the coach uses it too often. Eventually the runners may just choose the wimp road.

Indian Treadmills

I have no idea where the name came from; I just know that my high school cross country coach, Paul Wood, called them this. So I will too. Cyclists may know these as pace lines. I have also heard them called Indian files. Either way, the runners simply take turns leading. Perhaps, you divide the team into groups of five to 10. They are allowed to run anywhere they want, but must rotate the lead every so many minutes. Some leaders will run hard and fast, some will run slow. Some will head for the hills, and some away. It becomes fun, when the runners within the line have differing views of where to go and how hard. I have seen them head toward the hills, and away from the hills, toward the hills, and away. . .

There are two ways of changing the lead. You can have the runner from the back of the line surge up to the front, or the runner in the front drop off to the back. I like to assign the first method when I want them to run harder, and the latter when I want them to run easier.

Value: The Indian treadmill run can serve any form of workout during any phase of the season depending on how you structure it. You can even use it daily, if you like.

Follow The Fearless, Friendly, Leader

I devised this workout to make Indian treadmills a little more enjoyable. Follow The Fearless, Friendly Leader is basically the same thing. The difference is that I tell them that the leader is to be fearless and he is to run hills, go over things, explore new areas, run through bushes, etc. . . . Yet they are to be friendly in that they dictate a pace that all the members in the group can handle. The primary excitement to this workout is in the exploration of new territory, the varied terrain, hopping over logs, etc. At minimum there is the excitement of guessing where the leader will take the team to next.

This game can be great fun with large numbers. When I lead this game with my team of 25-40 I take them through sprinklers, jump over ditches, run figure 8s, etc. If all the runners remain in a single file line you can make neat-looking geometric figures too. For example, you can run in a circle of decreasing diameter.

I have used this workout with two groups, having the second group start one minute after the other, and telling them that each leader is to lead for two minutes, but at the end of each two-minute session the group must pass by me (who remains on a bench). The leader of that group then drops off at the bench with me and rejoins the group when it swings by two minutes later. This provides the coach with a minute or two of one-on-one time with each runner, without interfering with the workout. With two groups starting one minute apart, the coach is given essentially one minute with each athlete.

Value: Same as Indian treadmills, yet there is also the advantage of individual time spent with the coach.

Lewis & Clark

A similar idea to Indian treadmills was passed on to

me by Coach Greg Switzer of Hoover High School. It involves park running in which the leader can take his group wherever he wants, no matter how bizarre. The twist comes in the rules:

1. The group does intervals, in which the leader can set any pace he wants for a given time.

2. Upon the conclusion of the fast part, the leader must turn around and jog in the direction he just came in order to pick up any stragglers and re-establish the pack.

3. The group switches leaders at the start of each interval.

Value: Same as Indian treadmills, but necessitates fartlek-type running.

Devil-Take-The-Hindmost

Though I don't know who actually originated this game, it has been used at the L.A. Times and other indoor track meets. The concept is basic. The runners begin on the track and, as they pass by the lap mark, a guy dressed in a devil costume (complete with plastic pitchfork) jumps out and chases the runners. The devil stabs one of them in the butt. He normally stabs the last place runner, but the coach can change this if he wishes. The stabbee then drops out of the competition.

The problem with this game is that if it is played on a 400-meter track you could have a pretty long workout. Perhaps having two devils would work well for this situation, one at the 200 mark, the other at the finish line. Another problem is that the slower runners are usually stabbed first and they may be the ones who need the most work. Therefore you may want to handicap it, or allow the slower runners more than one stab.

Devil's costume optional—perhaps use a red ski cap or something else to identify the devil.

Value: This serves as a good tempo-paced or strength run. It is most appropriate in the strength phase of the season.

Last Man Out

Similar to Devil-Take-The-Hindmost, this game was suggested to me by Jim Stintzi, Cross Country Coach at Michigan State University. The athletes run a set distance, preferably off the track (say 300 meters), but run in a loop. The number of loops equals the number of runners in the game (not too many or they end up running too far). After the first loop, the last man to cross the finish line is out of the game. He continues running but goes around the loop in the opposite direction. The rest of the group continues (without stopping) into the second loop. Once again, the last man to cross the finish line is out of the game and must turn around and continue in the opposite direction. The game continues until there is only one man left.

This is a great race simulator, as those who are not very quick can extend their life in the game by starting out at a quicker tempo than the kickers. Likewise, the kickers can bide their time in the back of the pack and hope the front runners eventually come back to them. Requiring "eliminated" runners to run in the opposite direction means everyone keeps running the same length of time.

Value: Last Man Out provides a good tempo-paced or strength run. It is most appropriate in the strength phase of the season.

Search And Run

This workout takes some serious planning on the coach's part, but proves to be a good mental and physical workout. The workout is run much like a car rally. The coach gives each group, or the whole team, a piece of paper with the first clue on it. The team runs all over town, finding the clues that bring them to the next location. After running to many different clues, they find the winning certificate, or perhaps a buried treasure.

You can give each team envelopes with the answers to the clues on them, in case they don't get the clues. Tell them that points will be subtracted for each opened envelope. This workout demands that someone take charge and allows for good teamwork. Plan the course for complete safety, however, with a minimum of traffic and other hazards.

Value: This workout works well on easy days. It is designed to build teamwork and increase cohesiveness. As I said, though, it requires much planning on the coach's part.

Duck Duck Goose

Played just like the child's game, with the exception that the boundaries should be much larger. This game itself will not necessarily be considered a workout; however, it makes for a fun session to run to a park, play for a few minutes and run back.

Value: A fun game designed to increase team cohesion.

Pool Polo

Coach Medellin from Esperanza High developed this water workout for the team. Form two teams; all are wearing a wet vest or other flotation device. They play water polo just like the real game but must run to the ball. The coach must watch to ensure that the runners are using proper running form, and not swimming to the ball. I recommend using a soft ball to stop slow-acting distance runners from being pelted in the face by a hard water polo ball.

Value: Pool polo—similar to a fartlek session in the pool.

Mini-Olympics

This workout was given to me by my cross country coach in high school, Paul Wood. The coach divides the team into equal thirds, and presents each team with a list of different events. Each member is responsible to run or compete in one event, and no more. Points are awarded for each event for first, second and third places. The team captain of each team must figure out who will do each event to optimize his team's chances of winning. The teams then compete.

The coach may include other track and field events. You may even discover a jumper or thrower. Either way, you will find a supportive team cheering on each member. Of course, the losing team has to do pushups.

Value: Builds teamwork and cohesion. It is a good diversion from hard training. . . or monotonous training.

Predicted Time Runs

Another idea given to me by my coach, Paul Wood—you break up into two or more teams and collect all watches. Tell each team how many laps they must run. Allow them to predict a time that their team will finish in. They then run the specified number of laps without the aid of the watch. Tell them that the team that comes closest to their predicted time wins.

To add a bit of strategy to this you can allow the team to finish with a gap of no more than 10 seconds (or 20 or whatever) away from their predicted time. Whichever member of the team crosses the finish closest to the predicted time—his time counts as the team's time. If the gap is more than 10 seconds (if that's the preset gap limit), they are disqualified.

The runners will come up with unique ways of gauging time. The last time I played this game one team finished runners at 9:59 and 10:01 when the time to hit was 10:00. They did this by running to the track where they felt they knew pace. The other team; however, beat them, as they hit 10:00. Their method was to count strides per minute.

Another variation is to have them run these laps in relay fashion, without the aid of the watch. By allowing them to pick their own time, they can run as hard or as easy as they like.

Value: Predicted time runs function best as a way of making an easy day more interesting, though they can be used as strength runs as well. They help build the runners' kinesthetic sense of pace.

The Guessing Game

In this game the motivation is in knowing that it will be one of the hardest runs of the season. The concept is to tell the runners that they are going to run what coach says, when coach says it, and they will not know what the whole workout will consist of, or when it will end, until it's over. The coach should make each interval of different length and location. Keep them guessing.

By having the athletes run various distances for their repeats, and in a variety of methods and locations, it makes a hard workout more enjoyable. An example of the workout might look something like this:

1. Run from this pole to that sign hard.
2. Run hard for 30 seconds.
3. Give the slower runners a head start and tell them to run hard until the faster runners catch them.
4. Run to the top of that hill hard.
5. Run hard till I yell to stop.

You get the idea here, I hope. Just don't let the athletes know exactly what the workout will be, or what will come next. Or you can allow recovery after one leg and then ask them what they think will be next. "No . . ." "No . . ." "You got it!" As soon as the workout is guessed, they take off and do it.

Value: Depending on the directives the coach provides, this workout can be utilized for an easy day, the hardest workout of the year, or anything in-between. The main element is to keep the athletes guessing as to what will come next. In this it helps make a long workout seem shorter.

The Circle Game

This workout was taken from *Runners World,* and the inventor is Mike McGlynn of Michigan. Take two teams of 10 runners each (five on the track, five in reserve); compete in a four-quarter game. Each quarter includes four races, ranging from two to eight laps. During each race the 10 runners on the track don't know how far they'll be running *until the bell lap* because the head referee (coach) selects the distances.

They can take a chance and start fast, hoping the race will be short, or start slow and count on a strong kick. The race winners score points for their team on a 6-5-4-3-2-1 basis.

A two-minute rest period follows each quarter. During this period, teams can substitute fresh runners for the five who have just finished and, if necessary, call a one-minute time-out (only two allowed per half). At the end of four quarters, add up the scores.

Value: The circle game is a strength run. It develops teamwork and cohesion.

Bound-A-Round

Though I made up the name, I got the idea from Coach Bill Freeman at Grinnell College in Iowa. Many teams bound, but I was particularly impressed with the way in which Coach Freeman had his athletes doing it.

He has them bound down a runway for about 30 meters and then walk off at a quick pace and cover a half-circle back to the start completing the loop by bounding back down the runway. This made the exercise a nonstop one. You bound, walk, bound. The leader is the one responsible for setting the pace.

Additionally, Coach Freeman had his team bounding to upbeat music. It gave it all a sense of rhythmic dance. After I saw his team do this I thought I would try it with my team, expecting to meet with much resistance. Quite the opposite—my team loved it.

They can also bound for one song, peel off down the track for some buildups, and end a buildup by going right back down the runway for more bounding.

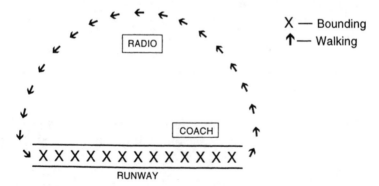

X — Bounding
↑— Walking

This workout gives the coach the ability to view and critique each athlete as he comes down the runway. It works much better than the traditional method of having the runners flank out, and it also gives the younger team members the chance to see the older ones bound. I place them in order: senior, freshman, junior, sophomore. This allows for optimal viewing of the experienced athletes.

Value: Bound-a-round is a way to improve the quality and enjoyment of a coach's existing bounding (plyometric) sessions. Each coach has his own ideas on how often, long, and fast to bound.

Team Intervals
Inspired by the "Minute Man" in cycling. The coach determines how much rest he wishes his runners to have between 400s. The runners then line up in single file, and the coach releases one every three, four or five seconds, depending on how many runners there are and how much rest he wants them to have.

When a runner finishes the repeat he returns to the back of the line and waits his turn again. This allows a precise amount of rest, and allows each runner to attempt to catch his "Minute Man". It also provides the coach with an opportunity to observe each runner's form and to discuss it with him.

The drawback to this run is that most coaches (myself included) recommend jogging or slow running between intervals.

Value: A variation on an interval workout (repeat 400s). Good to use periodically as something a bit different from the routine.

The Dipsea
Though I borrowed the name from the famous race, I received the idea of the workout from Phil Ryan at San Marino High School. Most coaches have their athletes do hill repeats during the strength portion of the season. The

traditional method is to run up, turn around and walk down. Phil suggests finding a hill that you can run up, walk down the other side, turn around and run back up. In this you create a circuit-type effect, and it allows the athletes to cheer each other on too.

Value: Hill repeats for strength.

Statue Of Liberty

Randi Rossi at Irvine High in Southern California says that his kids' favorite run is the Statue Of Liberty Run. The concept of this run is simple. It's an interval session in which the team is divided into two.

Group one runs hard for a prescribed amount of time while group two jogs. When group one's time elapses the leader thrusts his arm and closed fist into the air (like the Statue of Liberty) and this signals the second group that it is their turn to run hard. Group two passes group one, puts distance on them and throws their arm up when their pre-scribed time has elapsed.

For groups of unequal ability, give the slower group more time to catch and pass. You can also work this with three or more groups.

Value: An interval workout variation.

Pick Your Poison

In this game the coach writes various instructions on small pieces of paper that are handed to team members before a run over a designated course. The instructions will be known only to each particular runner. For example one instruction might read, "Surge up death hill" or "Run hard from 3 to $3^1/2$ miles." Start the game as an easy group run for the first mile or two to serve as a warmup.

As the first designated runner follows his specific

instructions, it's the job of the other team members to "cover the surge." The front runner has the advantage of surprise, and the knowledge of where the surge will go and how long it will last. The chasers are forced to decide how to pace themselves as they pursue. Then the second "leader" takes over, and so on. Be sure to allow a rest interval, too!

My runners like to signify it's their turn to push the pace by yelling "shaboom" and then taking off.

With a little creative thinking, the coach can handicap this game to account for varying abilities.

Value: Pick Your Poison is a great strength run into which the coach can program anything he thinks the team or individual runner needs to practice.

The Assassin
Randi Rossi has an interesting variation to Pick Your Poison in which the coach assigns a number to each athlete before the run. Each number has a time listed below it that he is to surge for. The athletes don't know when the coach will call their number. When the coach does, they must surge for the amount of time (or steps) that was given to them, as the others "cover the surge."

Value: Same as Pick Your Poison.

Indy 500

For this game the coach finds a small hill loop of 150-300 meters. He tells the team that this is going to be a race to see who will finish first. The coach staggers the runners, from slowest to fastest. The rules are that you must take a break for "X" amount of minutes/seconds (the coach decides). A runner can take his break at any point he wants. Or he can divide his allowable break time into two or more pit stops. The first one to complete the course wins.

I had my team do this workout once in the mud. Not only was it a competitive workout, just trying to win, but they seemed to really enjoy scrambling back up the mud hill. This workout can employ injured or sick athletes as timers and to tell the pit-stopped runners how much time they have left. You can also run it in two-member team fashion.

To make it fair, match the fastest runner and the slowest, the second fastest with the second slowest, etc., and allow a stagger.

Value: A hill workout made enjoyable and challenging. Run individually it serves as a tempo hill run; in teams it becomes a hill-interval workout.

Fox And Hounds

This game is borrowed from Tom Donnelly of Haverford College. Fox And Hounds, Haverford-style, basically means that the coach (the fox) gets a several-minute head start. The team (the hounds) sets out in hot pursuit of the coach. This game has also been called "Hares And Hounds" and "Run, Sheep, Run."

Mark Will-Weber in his article, "Games Coaches Play," describes a few twists to this workout. A good variation is "Rabid Fox." Once the original fox is caught, he turns on the hounds. Every hound he catches then becomes rabid and helps the fox chase down the other hounds, until all are caught.

You can also try "Free Fox" in which two or three of the faster team members are designated foxes and the rest of the squad hounds. The object is to tag all of the foxes, but

a tagged fox is still allowed to run around and can be freed again if one of his fellow free foxes tags him, returning him to liberty. Only a free fox can set loose a captured fox.

Value: This workout involves varied-pace running. It adds spice to a regular routine. Because of the chasing involved in the game, it does involve speed. It can be used during all phases of the season by modifying the boundaries and time of the game.

Time Bomb Repeats

Another idea by Mark Will-Weber, and an excellent way to teach pace. Split your team into various groups (according to ability) for their interval workout. For example, suppose the workout is to run 12 continuous laps in 85 seconds. Give them a "safety zone" of 10 seconds over or under their prescribed time. If they run too fast or slow on the repeat, they are penalized by adding 100 meters to the run. Signal penalties by a Whhhhh (a whistling sound). . . Booommmmm. . . from the coach (any noise the coach finds appropriate to get the message across). The first team to complete the run wins. Staggering, too, may be necessary.

To help teach them pace, *don't* tell them if they were too fast or too slow, just that they were off. I think this helps the runners learn to develop an awareness of pace faster than if the coach is telling them their specific times.

Value: Interval workout and pace judgment development with an added element of interest.

Pace Game

This is a pace teaching game from Coach Stintzi at Michigan State University. The game is run on a large grass area, preferably an open area. The coach gives the athletes the "go" signal. The athletes individually select a pace and destination to run toward. They run at a continuous pace until the whistle is blown—they then stop exactly where they are. The coach notes the time. Each athlete will probably be at a different point on the loop when the whistle is blown. When the coach blows the whistle a second time, the athletes turn around and attempt to run back at the exact same pace. The whistle is blown once more, with the same duration of time as before. The runner closest to the finish (start) line wins.

Value: The pace game can be used during any phase of the season by changing the duration of the runs. The coach can have his athletes run short and fast distances, or can tell them to run for 40 minutes, turn the watch off and return. It works especially well with young runners.

Whistle Workouts

Phil Ryan at San Marino High School in Southern California uses whistle workouts to make speed sessions more enjoyable. "They do the warmup, stretch, and then the whistle will blow and they don't know how long they have to run fast for. They will go all over the park or soccer field or wherever. I'll make up routes, and they alternate taking the lead. They don't know when the whistle will blow again. The leader decides where they go."

Coach's Dumb Decathlon

Coach's Dumb Decathlon takes some planning on the coach's part, but proves to be one of the most pleasurable, and funny, workouts I know of. You can make up any 10 events you like. Here is one suggestion.

First, I hand each team an envelope that tells them what the name of each event will be, how many points it's worth, etc. The letter also gives them a bunch of mundane instructions and at the bottom of the letter it says, "This letter is worth ten points if turned in to me at the end."

Event #1   Predict-Your-Time-Run: Give them a slow time. This will serve as a warmup, and allow you to take care of any "problems" so that you can concentrate on the rest of the events.

Event #2   A goofy relay (any one).

Event #3   Another goofy relay (any one).

Event #4   Still another goofy relay (any one).

Event #5   Coach, I Can't Run Because. . . Give each team two minutes to fill out the sheet with statements to be completed like, "Coach, I can' t run today because. . . " Or "Coach, I lost the race because. . . " Or "Coach, I missed my race because. . . " Read each team's responses and award points for the funniest, most creative, and so on.

Event #6   A straight, fast relay.

Event #7   A fast predict-your-time run.

Event #8   Search And Run. Something like "Your team has three minutes to collect the following objects. . . "

Event #9   A slow predict-your-time relay (warmdown).

Event #10   The Academic Portion. This envelope should include a test and a pencil. Ask them all kinds of questions. Questions about training, racing, physiology of running, whatever. I also like to include questions about our school's history or the team's alumni. Perhaps questions about the coach will work well; it may allow them to learn something about you, and vice versa.

Value: Same as goofy relays: diversion, team morale and cohesion.

The Passing Game

The passing game can be used as a strength or LSD (long slow distance) run. The runners must first know how to pass another runner effectively. (You may first want to read about passing in Chapter 3.)

The game works like this. You have the team pair up into partners of similar ability. You have them run for however long you want their strength run to last. One runner sets a tempo or faster pace, and holds the pace. The second runner starts ten seconds later. The second runner works to catch the first runner over time, gets in behind the lead runner and rests for a moment. The second runner then waits until an opportune moment to pass and does so quickly. He passes and puts distance on the first runner. Now the runner who was just passed drops back until he is 40 meters or so behind and then he works his way back to the lead again, and so on.

You can utilize this run while doing a tempo pace or while running slow and easy. I think the most exciting way to do this run would be to chose a tempo pace over a cross country course. This gives the runners a chance to think about not only how to pass, but when to pass, as well.

Another method of using this run would be that of a fartlek-type run. You would simply catch the runner in front of you with a hard effort, pass him and run hard for another 15 seconds. As soon as the runner is passed, he walks for 15 seconds. Then the leader jogs at a slow pace until passed, he walks 15 seconds and then goes hard again to catch up again.

There are actually a variety of methods to use for this workout. You could even do it in groups and have an Indian treadmill where each runner takes a pull to catch another group. Another possibility is to run it on the track and tell the runner that he has exactly one lap to catch up—no more, no less—and he must run a consistent pace. This teaches the runner to develop a sense of pace.

Value: The passing game is a way of making easy days more interesting at slower paces and can serve as a strength run at faster paces. Either way it teaches this particular tactic.

Pack, Pace and Passing Practice

For many runners it is difficult to remain relaxed and in control when they are running in a tight pack of other runners. By specifically practicing this situation the runners can simulate the racing environment and learn to protect themselves and relax in the pack situation.

Have the runners pack up tightly and maintain a steady pace while running around the track. This will get them used to pack running.

The coach can also teach "catching" skills by telling the

runners that when you call their name they are to drop out of the pack and slow to a stop, at which time they are to count to ten, and then accelerate to a constant pace that will enable them to catch the pack in one lap—no more, no less.

Once they catch the pack they are to wait until the beginning of a straightaway and then surge past the pack. After establishing a 30-meter lead, they are to slow down and rejoin the pack.

Value: This workout is a variation that works well on an easy day run. It teaches the athlete how to run in a pack, how to catch a pack, and how to pass a pack. It can be done on a cross country course as well.

Tee To Greens

Though I can not find the source of this unique workout, it deserves to be mentioned. On a local golf course, the runners run hard from the tee to the green, which is generally anywhere from 100 to 500 yards. The runners then jog to the next tee and then run hard to the next green, and so on. This provides for a nice grass workout, with varying repeat distances.

Value: Depending on how many holes are run, and at what pace, this can be a strength or speed workout. Either way it is run on the soft grass which helps to minimize injuries.

Golf On Fast Forward

Another workout from Mark Will-Weber at Moravian College in Pennsylvania, Golf On Fast Forward provides a great fartlek run. It is similar to Tee To Greens. The difference is that the runners carry a golf iron. They hit the ball and run to the ball. The object is for the team to complete 18 holes in as few putts as possible. The better the shots, and the faster the running, the sooner they will finish. If you are

concerned about the runners hitting each other with the balls (a real concern) a twist might be to have just the coach take the shots and the team runs to it.

The Hat Game

This game, another submitted by Rich Medellin, has each runner on the team bring a hat to practice—any type will do. The rules of the game are basically a glorified game of tag. One runner starts off as "it" and has his hat on; he must run and tag another runner. When he does so that runner must put his hat on and join the "it" runner or runners and will thereafter assist in the tagging. More and more runners get tagged until there's only one left—the winner.

Coach Medellin says that by setting large boundaries in this game it can last as long as 45 minutes. It can make for quite a good workout, "You are jogging to kids a half-mile away then you sprint after them and try to catch them." It is a great fartlek-type workout. "Usually you tag the slower kids first and they then chase after the faster kids. Eventually you have six or seven slower kids chasing the faster kid. It's a fun game. I think the runners like it when the coach starts off as 'it'. We usually end the workout with a watermelon feast."

Value, frequency: Fun, teamwork, fartlek. Similar to Fox and Hounds.

Quarter Mad

A common prescripton for strength runs is three or four miles of quality running. 12 x 400, 6 x 800, 4 x 1600, or a 3-4 mile tempo run are all examples of this.

Larry David at Hart High School in Southern California passes on a workout designed to determine what intervals can be run within that three or four miles. For example, the coach determines that he wants the athletes to run four miles worth of intervals and he wants them to be repeats between 400 and 1200 meters each. For each repetition to be run a designated member of the team flips a quarter three times. For each heads that appears, the runners will do 400 meters. In this fashion the runners keep flipping the quarters, and running, until they have run four miles of intervals.

The recovery for a workout like this can either be the same as the distance covered or it can be another designated amount of time. You can have the runners take turns flipping the quarter; that way the "blame" can be spread. It is easy to adjust the distances to whatever you want.

By adding more flips of the quarter you lower the distance each represents and increase the statistical probability of hitting a set distance. For example, if you wanted the bulk of the work to be predominantly 400s, have them flip eight times with 100 meters represented per flip. In this fashion you will see mostly quarters run, some 300s and 500s, and not much of anything else. Individuals can use this method too.

Team Pursuit

Team Pursuit is a game suggested by Coach Barry Sachs. Team Pursuit is a fartlek training run designed to provide the group with speedwork and the coach with the opportunity to view all involved.

Divide the team into groups of similar ability. On a designated loop one team (Team A) is given a short headstart (say, one minute). After the minute has elapsed, Team B is given a "go" command, and the B runners must run hard to try to catch Team A, which in the meantime has slowed its pace to a recovery jog. Team B is timed in how long it takes them to catch A.

Next, Team B is given a one-minute headstart and A must then catch B. The strategy inheres in the pace of the recovery jog. The faster a team runs the recovery jog the harder it will be for the other team to catch them. On the other hand, it will leave them less recovered, and it will take them longer to catch up when it's their turn.

Whichever team has the lowest overall catchup time (say, for five to ten catches) wins. This workout can be done with as many groups as you desire, or it can be done with individuals. In order to insure that one team is able to catch the other, you can handicap the better squad by adjusting their headstarts.

Rope-A-Dope

Coach James Acklin of St. Joseph Ogden High in Illinois is credited with this one (found in *Runners World's* 1995 *High School Runner*). Rope-A-Dope may be the ultimate hands-on pack running system. It teaches the runners to stay together in a pack, while giving the faster runners slightly more resistance than the slower runners. Basically, the runners are tied together with a rope to make sure they are not separated during the workout. Coach Acklin ties five to seven runners together at a time, using flag football belts and three feet of rope between them. He only does the workout on grass, in case runners fall. Mile repeats or tempo runs are the best ways to do this workout. It would be best to rope together athletes of similar ability.

Sandbag Run

Rich Bellante at Aliso Niguel H.S. in Southern California recommends this run for the purpose of building team cohesion and teamwork. The coach divides the team into groups of equal abilities. He gives each team a sandbag weighing about 10lbs. and tells them that the first team's sandbag to finish the (whatever distance) course will be the winning team. The runners may carry the bag in any fashion they desire, and may pass off or team up as much as they want. Each team member, however, must carry the sand for some duration of time. Upon debriefing you might talk about the significance of teamwork. Perhaps you could have the team's best runner do it alone; thus showing them the significance of just how much faster they can get a task done as a team.

Pen Relays

This relay event sees the runners doing more of a tempo paced run. Basically each individual gets a different color pen. The coach photocopies a sheet of papers with the clues as to the location of clipboards that the runners have to run to. Each runner must sign each clipboard and return back to the starting point. The runners can sign the clipboards in any order they choose. Perhaps by taking the time beforehand to determine the location of each, they can then determine the shortest route to cover them all. Give them, say, 10 minutes to work out the clues, then send them off.

An example as to a clue might be as follows. Let us say that you had placed a clipboard at the intersection of

Golden West and Garfield Streets. The clue might read something like: Clipboard #4 is located at the corner of Not Silver East but . . . and a cartoon cat. The older runners might even get harder clues.

The coach determines how far the athletes are to run by how many clipboards they have to sign and how far away the clipboards are. He can give headstarts or assign handicaps to give everyone a chance to win. Or the coach can simply have the slower runners run to fewer clipboards.

There are plenty of ways to vary this workout. Paul Mariman of Philomath High School in Oregon recommends letting the team decide who is going to go to what clipboard and just requiring one member of each team to sign a clipboard. In this manner the faster runners can run to the farther clipboards, and so on.

The Chalk Trot

Many track and field equipment distributors and running shoe stores now carry a spray-on chalk for marking courses. Andrea Johnson at San Gorgonio High School in California has one male and one female from her team each take a can of this chalk and gives them a five-minute headstart onto a new run to explore. Five minutes later the teams head out in pursuit of the leader. The boys follow one color, the girls another. The leaders are entitled to go wherever they please, perhaps up a big hill or through forests. The coach will pre-determine just how often the leader should leave a marker.

This run has many benefits. First, it forces the athletes to learn to follow the arrows. They learn to scan for them without "stressing," a technique they may need some day on a poorly marked cross country course.

More importantly, the chalk markings allows a team to explore new terrain and then be able to turn around and follow the markers back. Oftentimes coaches want the ath-

37

letes to have the thrill of exploring, but fear they will get lost or run too long. This method gives them a beacon home, and keeps them all going to the same place (as long as the leaders don't get lost, that is).

Tour De France

Some coaches use a bike/run combination for long distance runs. In this workout the coach splits the team into pairs and has the pairs run a set distance or time. The two athletes take turns riding the bicycle, while the other runs. Some coaches use this workout for interval training, though I discourage this. Bicycle riding does not supply an adequate recovery or warmup for interval training. This run is best used for continuous long distance runs. What it does is double the distance you can travel. If you normally run a ten-miler by doing five out and five back, you can now travel ten out before turning back.

Street Smarts

This run supplies a strength run that progressively increases the pace. The coach has the athletes run up and down parallel streets (actually, you can have them run up and down the same street or stretch of trail, if desired). The athletes are told to run the first street in a given time (say, 65 seconds); then, after a predetermined recovery period, they are to do the next street in 63 seconds, then 61, 59, 57, and so on. Therefore, in each repeat the same distance is run, with the pace gradually increasing, and the recovery time between each leg remains the same.

A fun twist to this activity is to give the group a series of streets to run up and down—say, 10th Street to 20th Street. Have them run each one progressively faster and let them use their watches to pace themselves. When they finish with 20th Street, give them the total time. Then collect the watches (so they can't time themselves) and have them run back. Ask them to try to do this part of the session in the same time (65, 63, 61, etc.). Whichever team finishes closest (in elapsed time) to their outbound segment wins.

You can run this workout on the track, if you wish. And you can also delete the recovery periods—or allow them every other street, and so forth.

II. Pool Running and Games for the Pool

Outside of running itself, I know of no other exercise more beneficial in terms of providing the runner with the necessary tools to be a better runner than running in the pool. Its value has been proven time and time again. Mary Decker set a 2000-meter world record after running in the pool for three weeks in 1984 (Bloom, 1991). Joan Benoit trained in the pool for months before she won the first Olympic women's marathon in 1984 (McWaters, 1991). Ibraham Hussein, Suzy Hamilton, Joe Falcon, Steve Scott, and scores of other elite runners have made pool running part of their training.

The way to approach this type of running is to find yourself a wetsuit top or a flotation device that will allow you to maintain your form. There are commercially available flotation devices that work and other forms that may work too. Personally, I use my SCUBA-diving wetsuit top. This is a 7mm wetsuit, which provides me with enough buoyancy that I can remain motionless and have my lip just above the water line. When I begin to simulate the running action, my body raises out of the water even more. Stay in the deep water so you won't stub your toes. When I refer to pool running I refer to deep water running—the feet never touch the ground.

The concept of water running is basic. Just run. Maintain the precise form in the water that you would on land. This action is in agreement with the principle of specificity. You are running! The resistance in water is 12-45 times greater than on land, depending on your speed (Bloom, 1991). By maintaining proper form, you are helping to maintain the neurological patterns that are required for loose and relaxed running form on land. This, however, is where our first problem is introduced.

It may not be as easy to maintain form as it sounds. The problem arises with the flotation device. If it is too thick in the arm pits, it prevents the arms from tracking in the proper pattern, thus improper form may be reinforced. One of my runner's bought a device that looks somewhat like a back brace and attaches around the waist with the bulk of the device riding on the small of the back. Unfortunately, it forces you to lean forward excessively. It is important that all aspects of form remain the same as on land, including the lean.

Once you find a flotation device that suits (pun intended) these purposes, the best way to work on form is to simply visualize yourself running. Constantly check your form and visualize yourself on the track. You'll probably find pool running somewhat boring. Turning on a radio or having a conversation with a coach or friend will help, but ultimately it is not as stimulating as running on land.

Water running, done properly, will help maintain cardiovascular fitness, form, muscular strength and endurance. It may also help in the preservation of sanity during injuries. The duration of the water run can be the same as a regular run. Two miles of running in the pool generally equates to three miles of running on land, according to a 1991 *Runner's World* article (Bloom, 1991).

Each and every type of land run can be mimicked in

the water. In addition to maintaining endurance, deep water running can help with your sprint form and speed. Roger Kingdom, 110 high hurdles world champion, used it before his 1989 world record. He believes water running increased his turnover rate and stride (McWaters, 1991).

To simulate intervals, simply run hard for the same amount of time as you would on the land. If you would normally run 10 x 400 in 70, then run 10 x 70 seconds hard. To simulate tempo runs, find a good rhythm and hold it for the same amount of time you would on a land tempo run.

OK, how about hills? Simple, put some extra resistance on your feet. Extra resistance? Yeah! Shoes! Lace up an old pair of running shoes. This provides extra resistance; add that to an extra lift of the knees and you nicely simulate hill running.

Still need more resistance? Tie surgical tubing around your waist to the outside of the pool, and pull. If all is done correctly you will find that your form is that of running; not of trying to remain afloat. Your forward progress will be slow. There should, however, be some forward progress. Remaining stationary would be indicative of attempting to remain afloat. There is a natural instinct to tread water, instead of running. Be cautious of this.

Consider adding water workouts to your training schedule not just during injury. Each individual runner has a certain mileage limit. Attempting to exceed this mileage can and will eventually result in injury. With the addition of deep water running you can reduce your pounding on the roads or track and increase your overall mileage while lessening your chances of injury. Many runners have reduced their road mileage by 50% while improving racing performance, according to McWaters.

It is important to have an adequate warmup and stretching first. You may consider easy running in the pool for ten minutes, then stretching; we lose body heat 20 times faster to water than we do to air. Therefore, it is easier to cramp in the water. If you do cramp during a water run, do not attempt to stretch it out, as this will activate the myostatic stretch reflex resulting in prolonged cramping. The best method is to squeeze the muscle and concentrate on relaxing it. You will then need to warm the muscle up.

Here are some possible games for the pool.

Pool Soccer

By playing the same positions in the pool that a soccer team does on the field, a coach is provided with the opportunity to have the better runners play the forward positions, requiring more movement, and the slower runners to play the more stationary positions, like fullbacks. This allows the whole team to get the same quality workout, yet it's still individualized.

Pool Hoops

Same concept as soccer, but this time get one of those Nerf basketball hoops and play like you normally would. You can get two hoops and play full court, or one for half court. A wet Nerf ball is a perfect weight sponge for expending some energy to get it into the hoop.

Three Flies Up

Just like the baseball game you may have played as a kid. The runners (run) in the pool, and the coach stands at one end with a light ball and hits or throws it out. The team then scrambles for the ball. Points can be deducted if the coach detects runners swimming, as opposed to running.

Merry-Go-Round Intervals

Have the team all run in the same direction for a period of time. The water will begin to flow in that direction. Then, after a good flow is established, reverse the direction. Have the runners circle in the opposite direction of the flow. This may also simulate an interval workout. The interval part is in trying to get the water going the other direction, and the recovery comes once the flow has been established.

Pool Poll

This activity simply helps keeps the runners' minds active while they do a distance workout in the pool. The coach asks questions with a yes or no answer (he polls them). The coach tells them that all those who think the answer is yes, are to run to the right side of the pool. Those who believe the answer no, to the other. The coach supplies the correct answer. Those who made the wrong decision have to run in the back of the pool. The process continues until a single victor emerges.

Pool Formations

Another time-killing activity. Have the team practice drill team-style maneuvers in the pool.

Duck Duck Goose

Same as on land (see p. 17). Works well in the pool. So do a variety of other childhood games.

Pool Relays

There are a number of relays that you can run in the pool. Simply choose one from the ones recommended for land relays.

III. Motivational Runs

Rain Runs

Find the puddles and splash through them. "Singing in the Rain." The purpose of this run is quite simply to get as wet as you can. Perhaps to have the team join in a few rounds of poorly orchestrated, Gene Kelly-style singing too.

Spotlight Run

This run was taken from a 1987 *Runner's World* article by Don Kardong entitled "The Games Runners Play." Don talks about seeing a spotlight somewhere in town and calling his friend and racing him to the spotllight.

Shopping Center Run

Have the team run through a shopping center. Tell all team members that as they run past the windows they must pick something out that they would get the coach for Christmas, or his birthday, or any other day. You wouldn't believe how many times my runners have told me they would buy me the pink negligee.

Pool Run

On a hot day, it is great to have the team run to a pool, swim, and run back. One of my runners suggested having the team do a distance run by running from one pool, jumping in, getting right out and running to another pool. By plotting out how many pools there are, public and private, available to the team and their location, the coach can devise a distance run of any length by just having the runners go from one pool to another. You might even have the parents leave drinks out for the team.

Beach Run

Run to the beach, lake or river; swim or run barefoot in the shallow water, then run back.

Yogurt Runs

Simply tell the team the day before to bring money, and then run to a frozen yogurt shop and back. The fun part is watching the freshman, who ordered a large with everything on it, trying to run back. The coach should be prepared to buy for anybody who can't afford it, or lend to those who forgot money. Otherwise they are likely to rebel against the workout.

Some runners might experience abdominal cramps from the lactose in the yogurt. This is an excellent learning opportunity for the coach to mention to the runner that perhaps he should avoid eating dairy products before races.

Concentration Runs

As you are probably aware, the ability to concentrate is essential in racing. One method of improving the ability to focus is the concentration run. This run is ideally done with at least one other runner. It simulates the type of concentration required in an actual race.

This workout may be done at any pace, but the faster the better. The object is to shadow the runner in front of you, and to stare at the back of his neck. Make sure your head is upright, chin up. Any deviation will cause a narrowing of the trachea and allows for less oxygen intake.

Stare at his back and envision a rope binding you to him, or a hook latching you to him. You couldn't slow if you wanted to, for you are connected to him.

Concentrate on this for as long as you can. The faster the pace, the more it simulates actual racing situations. Periodically bring your attention to your form and pace, just as you would in a race. If there is a wind, search out and hold the ideal windbreak.

While this run can be done at a slower pace, it makes it harder, for too many distractions enter your head. The faster the pace, the less attractive that girl in the bikini is! Whole teams, too, can do this run, by simply running in single file.

A modified version of the concentration run is possible while running alone. Either visualize a runner directly in front of you or concentrate on an object (like a mountain) far off into the distance. The ability to concentrate is the ability to block out extraneous input and think about one thing only, like the runner who blocks out the sounds of the spectators cheering during competition.

The best way to learn concentration while running is to concentrate while running!

A Pain Run

Since most of our perceived pain is simply an early warning signal as to the physical status of our bodies, we must normally (with the exception of a peak experience) run through a great deal of pain if we are to experience running success in a truly all-out effort. The value of running hard in practice is that a truly difficult practice run can make a race look easy.

To perform this lesson in pain, you must choose a race, or create a race (among the team members). We simply cannot push ourselves hard enough in practice, for there is

46

usually insufficient motivation.

We all know how our priorities change under strain. At the beginning of a race that age-group award seems very important, but when it comes time to kick for that award its appeal suddenly diminishes. These changing priorities make it very difficult to experience this pain lesson in practice; therefore you should seek out a race.

Not just any race, it has to be one of such difficulty that time means nothing; finishing place, or just finishing, is the only goal. It's a race which you will, in fact probably have to stop and walk to relieve the pain. It must be . . . uphill. It must be *all* uphill.

Find yourself one of those crazy races that starts at the bottom of some mountain, and climbs to the top. These races exist; ask your local running shoe store if you do not know of one. Or read your running magazines, as they frequently cover them.

The reason for the hills and altitude? To allow you the opportunity to run the risk of running into oxygen debt virtually every step of the way. To experience pain. Without these experiences, you'll never push yourself all the way or to the edge.

The race I use for this yearly lesson is one called "Run to the Top." Appropriately named, it is a 8.2-mile ascent to the top of Mt. Baldy in Southern California. The race begins at 6,000 feet and climbs to 10,064 feet. It is all uphill with a total of possibly 1,000 meters downhill or flat. The incredible grade, a 10% average, and the lack of oxygen, makes it so that you will enter oxygen debt very quickly into the race.

Unlike a flat road race where you can go out too fast for a mile before feeling a tad of pain, this race will let you know the instant you push too hard. To race this course is to learn ultimately how to push your body without redlining. Of course, like in any lesson you will make mistakes, and this is where you will learn.

You will push some parts of the race too hard and be forced to walk. Your calves begin to tighten and you know that they only have a few running steps left in them unless you walk. You monitor *that* feeling of pain and *those* symptoms that go with them and you know that those are the particular sensations for you that are indicative of an all-out or excessive effort.

This is why I call it a lesson in pain. You are provided with the opportunity to experience for mile after mile the exact type of pain, or level of pain, that goes along with an all-out effort. You quickly learn to say either, "OK, this pain hurts but I have lots of fight left in me" or "Now, this pain says that I am about to lose contractile ability."

Upon the completion of the race I take the opportunity to talk to the runners about the pain they experienced. Most all the runners I talk to agree that if they set a steady pace up a steady incline they felt a certain degree of pain, yet they could hold this pace for miles, and the pain did not worsen.

This common report supports my theory that pain is perceived earlier than is necessary; and that we can run through a great deal of pain at a constant effort without being adversely affected by it physiologically. Learning what his own ability is to withstand pain obviously benefits the runner.

By teaching ourselves our own body's pain signals we can learn how to set a pace that is close to the anaerobic threshold or redline, without pushing over it, and to hold this pace. Once this pace has been established we can then learn to disassociate from the pain so as not to feel it. Periodically we check back (associate) with ourselves to make sure our bodies are at the same position on the pain scale.

There is one final note in this lesson of pain. Running a race like the one mentioned will teach us to recognize and understand our body's systems of pain. Undergoing extreme, prolonged pain like this will put your normal racing life into perspective. The hill at the two-mile mark of that otherwise flat 5K will seem like a piece of cake. Very similar to the baseball player swinging two or three bats before hitting, we can teach ourselves that the pain is "nothing" compared to what I once endured. Ultimately your racing and confidence will prosper from this lesson; and that is what this run is all about.

Day Trip Run

Pack the team into a van and drive to an interesting park, beach, mountain or other running course. I do this with my runners two or three times a week during the off-season and try to do it at least once every week or two during the season. It breaks up the monotony of training around school and on the same track or courses.

I have also found that by naming the runs you go on the runners look forward to traveling to "torture hill," running hard, and then going out to eat afterward.

Train Track Run

Running on disused train tracks can provide for a unique running expereince. It can be challenging and teaches the runner to rely on his motor cortex for proper foot placement. But, basically, it's just a bit of fun. Every time I run with my team on our local train tracks, I feel like we are in a movie. You know, the kids walking on the train tracks and the song "Stand By Me" playing. I sing the words.

Watermelon Run

The coach starts the team off by giving them each a piece of watermelon and telling them that they must eat the melon and save the seeds in their mouths. The coach instructs them where to run to (less than a mile is ideal). They are told that once they get to the location they will be allowed to spit the seeds out at the coach.

Once they arrive, the coach tells them not to spit the seeds until the rules are heard. "You have only one minute to spit them at me. . . and you must catch me. . ." The coach takes off sprinting.

Watermelon is a filling food and this run will also serve the purpose of allowing the runners to feel what running on a full stomach is like. Some will have no problems with it; other will.

Planes, Trains and Automobiles

For some reason we tend to stick to our old running routes time and again. At the beginning of this chapter I talked about the thrill of exploring new ground. One way of doing this is to run to a mode of transportation for the trip home—to a bus, train or subway station or stop. Or have a friend drop you off "far" from home to run back. Teams can do this too. Have the team run to a bus stop 12 miles away, buy a soda at a store, and catch a bus back. Why not?

Punch and Cookies

This run is a community service and makes the runners feel good about themselves. Have the team run to a convalescent hospital or retirement home, where the coach has dropped off (ahead of time) refreshments for the runners. The residents can serve the punch and cookies to the team. This allows the youth to make positive contact with the older generation.

Dog Pound Run

For animal lovers. Have each member of the team bring a leash from home. Arrange ahead of time to have the local animal shelter allow your team to run to the shelter, each member takes a dog and jogs with the dog for ten minutes. The dogs will appreciate it and the runners will too.

IV. Other Things To Do While Running

Practice Tactics

There are lots of ploys a runner can use during a race to gain tactical advantage. Utilizing tactics during a race also serves as a form of disassociation from the pain. You can read about these in the next chapter, "Motivational Racing Tactics and Mental Games."

Practicing tactics in a workout is a pleasurable way of enlivening a normal run. Examples include playing the passing game, or practicing running to the front of a pack before a gate, playing with the windbreaks on an LSD run, practicing getting out of a box, and the like.

By practicing these tactics on the easy-day runs you are able not only to make the run more fun but you are actually teaching these tactics to your runners. The best method of learning is to do, and this serves the pupose.

There are at least 10 tactics discussed in the next chapter you can practice in a workout. This will make 10 easy runs more fun than simply just running somewhere. I utilize these tactics in the following manner. Say we are supposed to do an easy 30-minute run: I have the kids run 10 minutes to a park, we practice a specific tactic for 10 minutes, then they run back.

Modeling

Modeling is the simulation of the conditions that will be present on race day. You can either devise a race course of similar difficulty and layout, or have them run the actual course as a tempo run, or have them do segments of the course more than once.

Add Music

Any time you add music to a workout you'll get a favorable response. I play the radio while my team stretches and bounds daily. I also take three or four radios and put them around the track when we are doing intervals on the track, or up the length of a hill during repeats. Music releases endorphins, kills pain, and makes the run more enjoyable.

Form Game

This is a goofy concept in which one runner, during a run, apes the form of another runner. The team must then guess who the runner is imitating. There is some value to this in that it enables each runner to realize what minor variations of the running motion they are able to detect. It also clues some runners in to the fact that their form could be improved.

Card Games

On slowly paced runs the coach can bring a deck of cards. Deal out a card to each runner, and have them bet with pushups. After receiving their first card they can raise their ante. The dealer must cover all losses. Perhaps you can make a limit as to the maximum bet. At the end of the run everyone does his pushups.

You will find shuffling and dealing while running rather easy. I recommend you wear shorts with pockets in them for holding the cards of those who have "gone bust." Watch out for cheaters—they love to make big bets after they have switched cards with a friend. You can actually play any number of card games while running.

There are other unique things you can do with the deck of cards, perhaps you can shuffle the cards and deal them out. Each number can represent something, like the number of repeats you have to do, or the number of light poles you have to run.

Story Line

This is a conversational game in which the coach can start off by beginning the first line to a story. "It was a dark and stormy night." The next runner must then contribute the next line, and the next runner another line of the story and so on. The stories generally turn out be quite creative and humorous, and often (if you are running with boys) a bit risqué! Still, it's fun and helps to make the miles fly by.

COACHES: Remember to send us your ideas about other training games or creative workouts you have used successfully so we can consider them for the next edition of this book. Send to Training Games Editor, Tafnews Press, 2570 El Camino Real, Suite 606, Mountain View, CA 94040.

Chapter 3

Racing Tactics and Mental Games

I. Racing Tactics

"The race goes not to the swift, but to the wise." To the naive our sport seems a "no brainer." "Just put one foot in front of the other as fast as you can." Or as a coaching friend of mine, Jim Maynard, says sarcastically, "Run fast; turn left." The truth lies far from that. Racing tactics are just one tool in the spectrum of instruments the runner has available to him. There are opportunities to utilize tactics in every race, despite the course or distance. In fact, the longer the distance, the faster the pace, or the more obscure the course, the greater opportunity you have to use tactics.

Most runners know little about tactics and rarely use the ones they are aware of. Many are oblivious to the variety of tactics they can employ under differing racing situations. Some only concern themselves with pace, disregarding all tactical awareness. This is unfortunate, for tactics can help bring about both a better placing and a faster time.

Above all, tactics add spice to racing. They give you a sense of mastery over your sport. They empower you; giving you choices to make within critically short time periods. A good tactic here can increase your lead by . . . while a bad move can cost you . . . Fortunately, most tactics are risk-free—unlike strategies. What could go wrong with running a tangent, avoiding a box, or maintaining a break?

It is usually beneficial to plan your race strategy and to include the tactics you know will be beneficial into that strategy. Most of these tactics revolve around the course itself.

However, you must be ready to discard your original plan if needed. A change of weather, time, competitors, or qualifying standards are all reasons to change your strategy. Perhaps you would normally utilize the tactic of running the crown (middle) of the road during a marathon (where there is less of a slant) and race morning brings unexpected heat and humidity. It may be better to ditch this tactic and run the far side where shade from buildings and trees exists. Your tactical awareness has paid off.

I recommend practicing these tactics as part of workouts. This serves the purpose of gaining skill in the tactic and making the workout more enjoyable. Coaches will find practicing tactics a particular useful tool to make the easy-day runs more enjoyable for the team.

Wind

The wind is nature's varying method of ensuring that each race is unique. Work with it and you will profit, fight it and you will be defeated. The invisible molecules that make up the atmosphere account for 7-8% of the metabolic costs for running speeds of approximately 4:30 to 5:30 minutes per mile into still air (Cavanagh, 1990). That's a significant percentage. If you could run in an environment with no atmosphere you would be able to save a recognized 2-10% of your metabolic energies, depending on your speed. This would amount to a 2:18 time decrease for the duration of a 10K race, at a 5:30 pace.

Keeping a windbreak will not eliminate all of the air molecules you must push out of your way, but it can, however, reduce the amount by up to 80%. This 80% reduction can be obtained by trailing one meter behind another runner, effecting an energy reduction of approximately 6% (Cavanagh, 1990). Even at two meters back you still save 40% of the resistance or 3% of your total metabolic energy. Still, this two meter spacing results in a 1.42 second reduction per lap on a 400-meter track (Cavanagh, 1990).

As the wind speed grows, so do the advantages of a windbreak. Trying to determine exactly how much you save on a windy day is a mathematically difficult matter, however.

The following chart roughly indicates the percent increase for differing wind levels and the numbers used to come up with that percent. Keep in mind that these numbers only reflect the approximate percent increase in effort needed to maintain the same speed into the wind. They can also be utilized to determine what decrease in time would be expected for an all-out effort into the wind. These numbers do not include the standard 5-8% of your metabolic energies to overcome still-air resistance, simply the added headwind resistance. You will see that a one-mile-per-hour headwind is reported at .0068% and you must add this to the 7% required to overcome still-air resistance. Thus your total energy requirement to overcome the air resistance and headwind is 7.0068%.

Wind M.P.H.	Wind Meters/Second	% Effort Increase
1	.44	.0068%
2	.89	.056%
3	1.34	.192%
4	1.78	.448%
5	2.23	.88%
6	2.68	1.6%
7	3.12	2.4%
8	3.57	3.6%
9	4.02	5.2%
10	4.44	7.2%
11	4.91	9.6%
12	5.36	12.4%
13	5.81	15.6%
14	6.25	19.6%
15	6.70	24.0%
16	7.15	29.2%
17	7.59	34.8%
18	8.04	41.6%
19	8.49	48.8%
20	8.93	56.8%

As you can see, a headwind can be quite detrimental to your final time. Unfortunately, we also know that you will only gain back 50% of what you lost running into a headwind, when that wind is at your back (Cavanagh, 1990). So running a race on the track during a windy day, as you have undoubtedly already observed, will result in slower times.

An example of this can be shown in the following manner. If we normally run a five-minute mile on a straight road on a no-wind day, we can expect to run *approximately* a 5:19 mile into a 10 MPH wind the entire mile (5 x 60 x 1.072/60). Thus we would lose 19 seconds due to the wind. On a track, however, where the wind is at our back for half the race, we can expect to gain back half of that 19 seconds (8.5) and we can expect to run 5:08.5.

It seems obvious that keeping a windbreak would be beneficial while running into the wind. However, to most runners it does not seem obvious to keep a windbreak when the wind is at your back. Yet that is exactly what you should do. By constantly remaining behind another runner you will reduce your headwind by 40-80%. Then when you round the corner, or change directions to where the wind is at your back, you will be pushed by the wind and will be blocking the beneficial effect from the runner ahead of you.

Essentially, this is free energy for you and the guy in front will not profit from it. What a dose of double bad medicine. Not only does the guy in front have to break the wind, he doesn't get pushed by it.

The above discussion suggests that the ideal racing strategy for a track race, on a windy day, would be to maintain a windbreak the entire way. Finding a windbreaker who is running your pace, and one who picks the pace up into the wind and slows with the wind at his back would be to your advantage. All of this would serve to tire your opponent considerably and leave you feeling relatively fresh. Of course you're not often lucky enough to find the perfect windbreaker the whole race (until you're ready to kick).

Sometimes the ideal windbreak is not directly behind another runner. It may be best to move to one side or the other of the runner. If the wind is at your direct right or left it would be appropriate to move to the side of your opponent.

Finding the windbreak is easy to do. You can detect when you are deriving maximum benefit from the break not only by your perceived effort but by the sound of the wind. Practice will help you determine the pitch differences in sound from being behind the break or not. Be sure to leave enough room to avoid being tripped; take the opportunity to focus on your opponent and let him do the mental work.

Hills

Despite a runner's option to reduce or increase pace to compensate for variations in terrain, a hilly course is obviously more costly in terms of effort than a level one. In one study men ran on a 6% incline (six meters of vertical climb per 100 meters of horizontal distance) at an 8-minute-mile pace; they consumed 35% more energy than they did during level running (Costill, 1986). Running down the same grade, however, only reduced the energy demands by 24%.

This equates to a total of 11% more energy required for a course with equal uphill and downhill distances, providing that the grades are also equivalent.

You can learn, however, to utilize hills and grades to your advantage. Runners and coaches are largely misinformed about hill running tactics. They often believe in the myth of "charging hills." Typically you see a runner maintaining a steady pace, hit the base of the hill, and sprint up it. At the top he experiences considerable oxygen debt and "dies." His pace then drastically slows. Other runners easily pass, for when you "charge" a hill, you put it on your oxygen debt card with serious interest.

To take best advantage of hills you should remain relaxed running uphill, putting no extra effort into it than you did on the flat. Once you approach the crest of the hill feeling relatively fresh, increase your pace. You will catch your opposition with ease, and will gain immediate and substantial distance.

This is only half the story. Usually after an uphill section there comes a downhill. Once you have passed and gained distance on your opposition you will be able to further increase that distance by flying down the hill.

Why can't he fly the downhill too? Because his difficult effort up the hill has fatigued his muscles, causing them to tighten up which prevents an increased stride and turnover rate. Fatigued, short strides cannot extend far enough or rapidly enough to facilitate gravity's push. You know that when you desire to slow down while descending a hill, you take quick short strides. Your opposition is doing the same and it drastically slows them.

You now know that you can utilize hills to your tactical advantage in a race by cruising up them, moving on the top, and flying the downhill. However, there is more to know that will allow you to further distance yourself from your opponents: hill bounding.

Hill bounding is a straight-legged action, much like repeatedly bouncing on your toes. Hill bounding is a form of muscle contraction which stores the impact and returns it, much like that of a dropped rubber ball or spring. Bounding up a hill can save you 30% to 40% of your oxygen consumption (Cavanagh, 1990). Bounding up a hill will allow you to use less metabolic energy in reaching the top, thus making it easier for you to run harder on the downhill.

You may find that it is best to alternate a normal hill running style and a bounding style to utilize different muscle groups. Though this will decrease your total gain on the uphill it will allow for a longer stride and increased gains on the downhill as it needs all muscle groups as fresh as possible. Once you hit the downhill you should open up your stride and fly forward, using as much of gravity's help as you can. Landing on your toes will help ensure that you brake as little as possible.

Using And Avoiding The Box

Boxing is something that we generally think of simply in terms of avoiding, but we rarely think of using a box to our advantage.

First the explanation of the box. Being boxed (classically) is when you have the track's curb on your left, a runner in front of you, to the right side, and maybe one behind. Running in this position is dangerous because you are forced to run the pace of the people around you and you cannot escape the box without drastically slowing and going around, physically breaking through, or hoping an opening quickly develops. The danger is especially high in short distance races, where it is easy to be boxed in and not be able to cover a break or kick freely to the finish.

Usually, you want to avoid being boxed. To do so you are best advised to run just off someone's shoulder, allowing an escape, if needed. For short races, it may be best to avoid running the inside lane, especially near the start. Scanning

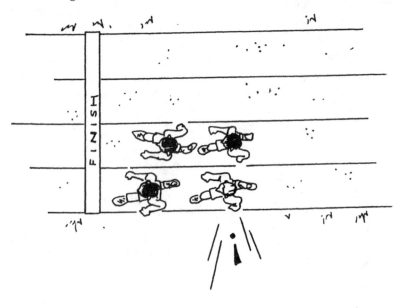

the runners ahead and observing what they are doing will help you avoid the box. Even being cautious of the box, you are bound to get caught in one occasionally.

If you are boxed in you need to think quickly. If the race is early it may make no difference. However, if you need to get out, either because the front pack is taking off, or because you need to begin your kick, you had better get out. There are several ways to get out of a box.

The first and often a highly effective way is to ask. "Scoot over, please" or even "I'm coming through" should work. Or you could try pointing between the guy on the right of you and the guy in the front and say "coming through." Or you may also decide that the race is early enough so that you can slow down a bit, and then move to the outside.

Lastly, you can, if absolutely necessary, try a braver maneuver of either attempting to squeeze through a small space on the inside of the track and pass the runner in front of you, or pushing your way through the gap between the guy in front and at the side of you. Be careful though—these maneuvers could get you disqualified.

We rarely think of using a box as a tactic, but if, for example, you see one of your opponents drafting off another on the inside lane, you can choose to pull up alongside him and remain there. Your purpose would be to prevent him from picking up the pace, pursuing a front pack, or kicking. Obviously the only reason you'd want to do this would be when you are sure you can out-kick this opponent.

By employing this tactic you will be sacrificing something. You may not be running the pace you wished to, and you will be forced to run the second lane around the curves. You must make the decision as to whether the benefits outweigh the drawbacks. If a boxed athlete asks you to let him out, always oblige. You are attempting to utilize tactics to run wisely, but use tact and be fair about it.

The last thing to be discussed in boxing is to know that you can be boxed anywhere, anytime. You may consider yourself boxed if you are in the middle of a pack during a marathon, but this is not normally a problem in races of such length. Make sure, however, you are able to pick up your pace, or pull out suddenly, if need be, in shorter races.

Gates

Sometimes, especially in cross country, you may run a race that passes through a gate or similar narrow path. Here lies both a problem and an opportunity. Consider this: if you are in a pack of, say, six runners, and you approach a gate with only room for one person to pass at a time, the pack will have to stop and wait for each runner to pass through individually. This results in a huge distance gain between the first and last one through. If you were in the back of a six-man pack, you may actually only be 10 meters or less from the leader, certainly within striking distance. Once you pass through a gate, however, you might find yourself 40 meters or more from the leader.

So, if you know of an approaching gate, you'd be wise to slowly surge to the front of the pack, attempting to be the first through the gate. This will automatically give you considerable distance on the runners behind you. If you approach your surge in an inconspicuous manner, people will think little of it. You should pass without problem. It may be an error to suddenly pick up the pace, as if you were taking off, because the other runners might react by doing the same, and you might find yourself in a sprint for the gate.

It is always to your advantage to know a course well. In the case of gates, familiarity with the course would allow you to take the lead before the gate is in sight, and the others would let you do it for they wouldn't know a gate was approaching.

Smart Gate Strategy

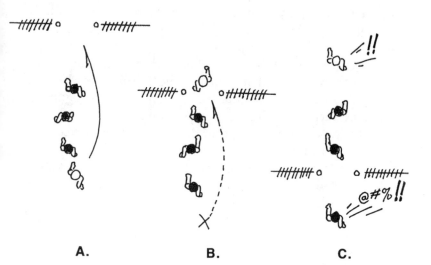

A.   **B.**   **C.**

Surging

Surging is simply throwing in a burst of speed some-where in the race. It can be an effective tactic to discourage a weaker runner. It is also effective in taking the kick out of a sprinter. Surging, however, is demanding on one's own body, especially if you have to break the wind as well. Without question surging is the hardest way to run a race. It makes the race that much more difficult.

There are specific times when a surge is definitely recommended. For example, you should definitely surge into a headwind in order to catch a windbreak if it is to your advantage to have a break. And you should certainly surge to weaken or discourage an opponent with a stronger kick. You can also utilize surging when desiring to keep another runner from using you as a windbreak. Or you can surge out of a pack into the lead and put distance on them.

There are times when you are absolutely advised not to surge. For example, it would be foolish to attempt to surge past runners on the first lap in the fifth lane of a two-mile to take the lead. It can be fatal to surge uphill when there is a long downhill following.

If you desire to surge past another runner, you'd best wait until you detect a sign that he is tiring. Perhaps a tightness in form, a momentary lapse of pace or an "ugghh"— and then surge past him. By doing so you will be surging past him during a mental low point during his race; chances are he will not pursue.

If you detect no sign of fatigue in your opponent, then you may wish to wait until either you can observe him turning his head to look at something on one side of the road; then pass him on the other side. Or you can wait for a runner or pack of runners to pass and hop in with them, let them pull you for a while, and then drop back to your pace.

Surging in pairs is mentally devastating to another runner. You may look toward your teammate, or even a non-teammate, at your side and indicate to him that you are going to take off and surge past him on either side. When two runners pass it has more of a negative effect on the one being passed. When you and a teammate pass an opponent on the track, do it side-by-side; this gives your opponent less time to react and pursue the windbreak.

If you are utilizing a runner as a windbreak, and that runner attempts to drop you by surging, you probably should try to match his surges stride for stride. Hang right on to him, he is not only tiring from the surges, but from the wind as well. If there is no wind, or it is at your back, you may decide to smooth out the surges by running a slightly faster but steady pace. Always try to stay with a surge during the final stages of the race.

If you are attempting to lose someone in your draft by surging then you should do the following. Surge once, hard, and then resume pace. He will be expecting a delay before the next surge, so take advantage of this and go hard within seconds again. This provides your best chance to drop him.

Tangents And The Quickest Route Possible

In cross country the course is the quickest route possible between markers, unless otherwise marked or indicated. Do not assume that you have to go around a tree, or stay on a path unless it is indicated to do so. Arrows do count as markers. It is the ultimate responsibility of the runner to know the course, even if it is not marked.

It's to your advantage to study the course before the race. Look for the quickest path, which may not always be the shortest path. For example, one of the courses I frequently race has 15 meters of a dirt-and-gravel hill, followed by 200 meters of gradual downhill dirt. You can, swing wide on the corner that leads up to the hill, where the dirt is more compact, and then run on the street as opposed to the dirt. This does require you to run 12 meters extra, but you save perhaps three by running up the hill on the harder packed dirt, and then you save your nine meters plus, by running the fast blacktop as opposed to the loose gravel.

Runners are often afraid to cut that tree or run off the side of the road for fear of being disqualified. It should be your goal to run the absolute shortest route possible without cheating. This is not even a form of minor cheating; it is simply being intelligent and finding ways to beat the course, rather than letting it beat you.

Tangents are one example of running the shortest route

possible. A tangent is taking the angle that will yield the shortest route possible. For example, if you were running down a street that had a succession of curves from the right to the left, you would be best to run straight down the middle of the road rather than following the curves. Running the tangents may also mean running from the apex of one curve to the apex of another.

When racing on a track, it is usually advisable to stay to the inside lane as much as possible. Remember that you will run 18 extra feet per lap by running the second lane. You can also save distance at the start of the 1500, 3000 or at the break of the half-mile by running a straight line from the break to the top of the curve.

1-2-3 Go

I find it helpful, especially in cross country, for a coach or friend to stand on the top of a hill or other strategical locations and yell to you, "1-2-3 Go." At which point you are to break out of the pack and pick it up. Having someone else tell you when you are to move often helps you execute what you know you ought to do. Yelling "1-2-3" works better than just yelling "Go" because it allows you time to prepare in your mind that you are fixing to go.

My runners say it works well when they are tired. Experience has proven to me that if I tell my runners to pick it up at the top of the hill as part of their strategy, some do and some don't, but if I stand at the top of the hill and yell "1-2-3 Go," all of them pick it up.

Catching Up

We sometimes find ourselves in the position of having to catch another runner or a pack of runners. If there is considerable distance between you and the runner(s) ahead, catch up slowly, unless there is a strong wind in which you may want to surge to quickly catch the break.

When catching up slowly, start by first setting your sights on his feet. Stare at them and draw them closer to you. He will, in time, come back to you. This method is more economical and involves less expenditure of effort than surging quickly to catch up.

When you have pulled him in close enough, you will find it necessary to switch your point of focus onto his butt. Otherwise, as you grow closer your head will necessarily lower to maintain that focal point on his feet and you will be decreasing the size of your thorax, reducing your air intake. Stare at his butt, and simply bring that butt toward you. As that butt grows closer, again change your point of focus to his neck, and stare at the back of his neck. Pull right up behind him, and continue to stare at that neck. Now you need to decide whether you want to stay there and rest, utilizing the windbreak, or to pass.

Staying Behind

Once you have reeled in an opponent and have decided to stay behind him you can employ a mental tactic to hold onto your position. I recommend staring at the back of his neck and visualizing a rope or a hook binding you to him. You couldn't drop off the pace if you wanted to, for you are connected to him.

The use of an affirmation will also help. Saying to yourself, "Loose and relaxed, stay on his back" or "Focus on his back, remain relaxed" are two useful affirmations for this situation. If the pace is intense you may also exercise mental tactics of dealing with the pain associated with that pace. You may say to yourself, "If I'm tired, imagine how tired he is breaking this wind," or "He will die any second." Still, concentrating on deep breathing and form will further your effort.

Passing

When you pass another runner, in any race, or at any distance, you are most always advised to do so with speed. If you slowly pass an opponent, he is liable to latch on behind you and use you for a windbreak. If you pass an opponent quickly, chances are he will be broken and not pursue.

When passing in a track race, you should almost always avoid passing on the curve. If you must pass on the curve, do so quickly and get back into the inside lane. Always look to make sure that you have a stride and a half (about seven feet) before cutting in.

Remember that passing is a psychologically destructive tool that you can wield on an opponent. Passing is always best when it will put additional negative thoughts into your opponent's head. For this reason, sometimes, depending on how you feel, it may be best to pass at a time when he does not expect it. The optimal time is when your opponent is undergoing psychological strain.

To detect this strain look for signs: a slight decrease in pace or a tightening of form. Other indicators include looking behind, a rolling of the head, the arms rising up, not running a tangent, landing more flat-footed or on the heels.

I have seen one runner pass another on the other side of the road. This is a psychological ploy—you pass without the other runner quite realizing it, and without allowing him to utilize you as a windbreak. This tool especially works if there are runners between you and he cannot see you sneak past. Rod Dixon won the 1983 New York City Marathon using this tactic, as Geoff Smith did not see or hear him coming.

Pressing And Psyching

Pressing simply means running close behind another runner. In actuality, it is drafting with the difference that you are just to the side of him, and you are as close as possible. Be sure not to impede his progress by hitting him, but make sure he knows that you're there. This will often make him grow worried, tight, or nervous—you are getting to him psychologically.

Once you have pressed your opponent, it may help to put some added heat on him. Say something like, "Fun race, eh?" or "Looks like a fun hill coming up" or "Not so bad, eh?" Imagine the psychological impact of hearing someone at the 22-mile mark of a marathon say, "What an easy course eh?" Where does this guy find the energy to talk? He is much fresher than I. He must not even be working. He is going to beat me. All of a sudden this little psych game has worked. One of your jobs is to make the other guy think you are better than he is.

It is important to understand that it takes no extra metabolic energy to blurt out a few short words. Talking is simply a matter of exhaling, with a little vocalizing. So feel free to talk. Just be careful about what you say. The right words can make your opponent doubt himself, the wrong words can add the extra incentive he needs to beat you.

The Reverse Psych

Since we recognize an "aughhh!" as a sign of fatigue, you can make use of this common knowledge as a form of reverse psychology. When you want someone to pass you and take the lead (so you can do the drafting), let out an "augghhh!" and slow a little; the runner behind will think you are too tired to maintain the pace and will probably pass. When he does, tuck in behind him and use *him* for a windbreak.

Running Through Sand

Sand is difficult to run through, so you are best to avoid it if possible. Sand allows your heel to sink down, forcing you to expend considerable energy to pull the foot out. This also

71

strains your calves and hamstrings. Therefore, go into the sand with momentum and attempt to keep your speed up all the way through it. Landing on the toes and rebounding quickly will help prevent you from sinking excessively into the sand. Keep a short stride so that you can get out quickly.

The Road

There are several factors to consider in determining what side or part of the road to run on.

- Tangents—what is the shortest route possible?
- Footing—which part of the road offers the best footing?
- Crown—how curved is the road; where is the flattest area?
- Lines—the painted lines on roads are sometimes slippery.
- Shade—where is the shade; do you need it?
- Wind—which side of the road is better protected?
- Cheerers—the closer to them the more they feed you.
- Opposition—where are they? Should you pass on the other side of the road?
- Water—which side of the road will the water stops be on?
- Cars—if they are on the course, run on the left side of the road so that you can see them coming and make eye contact with the drivers.

Use Of The Watch

The watch is a valuable tool during distance running. Knowing your splits can help you pace yourself over a longer distance. A watch can help you to go out at a reasonable pace or it can tell you your last mile was too slow, so you'll want to pick up the pace.

However, the watch is not always your friend. Occasionally we see a split and think to ourselves that the split is "too fast"; we then slow to meet our perceived appropriate pace. In doing so you may be cheating yourself out of a better performance that day.

In no way do I recommend disregarding what the watch says. I am simply saying that the more experienced you are at listening to your body's signals of perceived effort, the better you will be.

Knowing your splits is only one advantage of the watch. Get a watch that has a continuous countdown and pre-set splits. You can use the countdown to set it for 2:00 or 2:30 and then every time it beeps put in a surge. You can condition yourself in practice to do this during competition. Your pickups can become an automatic, conditioned habit.

Another feature of some watches is that of an extensive memory. My watch, for instance, has the ability to recall thirty splits. This means that I don't have to remember every 400 time during a workout, or every mile split of a marathon. Your watch may also average your splits for you. Thus you can know your average pace at the end of a race instantly.

The most common mistake I see, regarding the use of the watch, is when runners move to stop their watch just as they hit the finish line. When you reach for your watch, you slow down, because your arms are no longer driving. Chances are increased that you could be passed while you are fumbling for your watch.

The Finishing Kick

There is a myth regarding the finishing kick. "You didn't race hard enough because you had too much left at the end." To say this is not only incorrect but an insult to a runner who worked hard all the way through the line. You can almost always kick. Get up on your toes, and go.

Most of the time it is simply a mental thing. What happens is that we see the finish and grow excited, bringing about an insulin release; more sugar is absorbed in the cells, and we dig in and kick. To say that the only way a runner runs all-out is by collapsing exactly at the finish line is a joke.

To improve your finishing kick you may find it beneficial to run on your toes, then flat-footed, as far back as with a quarter left in your race. This will insure speed over the last stage of the race, not just the last 100m. It is much the same as surging; you simply run on your toes from four to ten steps, then drop back down to flat-footed. Then drive the arms hard for four to ten steps, then push with the ankles for four to ten steps, then lift the knees for four to ten steps, then the toes again.

Once you are within kicking distance, you must decide which type of kick to use: either a jump (a sudden acceleration) or a long, extended kick— then do it. You can do it; you can hold it. Remain relaxed, drive the arms, lift the knees, and above all remember that the pain of the race is nothing compared to pain of knowing what you could have done.

Starts

The start of any given race will depend on how many teams are in the race, and how wide the start area is. A coach can make strides/buildups more enjoyable by simulating a race start, as opposed to just doing strides or buildups. When teaching runners about starting, make sure they know to pay attention to three crucial factors: know the shortest route possible, know where the pack may funnel up, and have the fastest men line up first.

Cornering

You can make distance on your opponents by learning how to take corners properly. The first trick is to accelerate through every corner and to take four quick steps after you exit each. Most runners tend to slow down through corners and then pick up the pace to resume their original pace. Therefore, as you pick up the pace through the corners, you will not only gain the difference between your original speed and the increased speed, but you will add the distance that your opponent slowed through the curve. If you do this corner after corner, you will gain considerable distance. Furthermore, your opponent will not detect your speed increase, as he can not see you on the other side of the corner. As he rounds the corner he will see you running with the same intensity and will most likely not detect the few meters you gained on him.

For sharp corners it's best to slow down before you arrive and then to accelerate out of them. If you don't slow down chances are you will swing far too wide. This is especially true of those dreaded turnaround points. A successful method is to approach it in the same manner that a race car driver does. Approach from the far outside, then aim toward the apex of the corner. What this does is allow you to make the curve with as little turning as possible. Practice will help you determine what the fastest form of cornering is at any given speed or slope.

Dr. Michael Sachs at Temple University recommends that runners utilize corners in surging. He suggests that if you surge right after rounding a blind corner the opposition will not see you. If they don't see you they are less likely to respond to the move. In this fashion, with short surges through and after the curve, you can slowly add distance between you and the runner behind you, without him being aware of it.

II. Mental Games

This section is devoted to helping you run faster and enjoy it more through mental "games." Most of these are differing forms of visualization. Some will help you deal with pain, some self-confidence, and some just help to fill the time.

Relive The Moment

To relive a time in which you felt superhuman, a time when things came off precisely as you wished them to—a dream time–reviving the moment (or click back/click up) is the simple process of thinking back to a time in which you felt the desired way, and to come back to the present with that emotional attachment to the memory. When we store a memory, we attach to it an emotion. You can easily sadden yourself by remembering the loss of a loved one, and you can easily feel supercharged, gain power or confidence by remembering a time in which you felt empowered.

When things are rough, the pain high or the pressure on, it can help to "relive" a prior time when you managed similar obstacles successfully. Remember this time, and come back to reality with that emotional attachment. The idea is to have your current performance follow accordingly.

See The Outcome

During difficult parts of the race, when the finish line seems so far away, it is helpful to visualize the end of the race. See and feel yourself finishing in sensational time. Feel the glory that goes along with that finish, hear the crowds, feel the pride! I like to visualize myself having a great finishing kick—kicking faster to the crowd's delight, seeing the clock tick off the seconds as I approach my goal.

Toes, Knees, Arms

I utilize this technique during the last mile of a 5K in particular. It helps me to maintain the pace and forget about the pain I'm in. I basically focus on three aspects of form. I learned it from my flight instructor who always said to me (on approach to landing), "Glideslope, line up, air speed." The point was to empower the pilot so *he* lands the airplane instead of the airplane landing itself. I adapted it to toes, knees, arms.

Basically all I do is concentrate on getting up on the toes for, say, 20 seconds or so, and I just repeat to myself, "toes, toes, toes..." Then I get off my toes (since I can't run on them that long) and I concentrate on knee lift, "knees, knees, knees." Then I switch to arms. "Drive the arms, drive the arms, drive the arms." This empowers me and keeps my mind focused on maintaining the pace through form manipulation rather than effort—which allows me *not* to think about the pain.

Surge Alarm

A coaching friend of mine, Bill Summers at Corona Del Mar High School in Southern California, sets his watch countdown to go off every five minutes. When the alarm sounds he picks up the pace for one minute. Runners often find this form of motivation more useful than just telling themselves that they need to surge or pick up the pace.

It is sort of like having a coach tell you to pass someone or to pick it up, compared to trying to do it yourself. It may just give you that little extra incentive. Of course, one should be sure that a surge is appropriate when the alarm sounds. It may be devastating to surge up a hill, for instance, if that is when the alarm sounds.

Break Up The Distance

During difficult times of the run or race it is beneficial

to break up the distance into segments. Perhaps saying to yourself aloud, "just one more mile." Or looking ahead to the next street pole and saying, "just to the next one." Of course, once you get to the next one you need to say again, "just to the next one."

I find it easier to go on an hour-and-a-half run by fooling myself. Rather than saying, "OK, here goes the first minute of an hour and a half," I say, "Think I'll run 30 minutes and get a short workout in." Then when I hit 30 minutes I say, "45 is a much better workout and it only takes another 15 minutes." At 45 minutes I convince myself that "an hour looks much better in my log than does 45 minutes." Of course at an hour I say, "Heck, I've come this far; might as well go for all the marbles."

Dealing with time in this manner will help your racing too. It is often better to say to yourself, "only six more minutes," than it is to say, "only one more mile." Often the minutes seem more manageable than do the miles.

Taking Roll

Bob Messina, former coach at University High School in Southern California, used to have his team "take roll" at a designated point in the race. The purpose of taking roll was to keep the team together until a designated mile mark, at which point the leader would say, "Roll Call." Each runner in order would call off his name. Discouraging to the opposition, yes; it also builds collective efficacy in your team.

Key Word

Teams can have a code word to mean something like "let's go." Rather than having the coach say, "go now," which tips the others off to expect a surge, the coach can yell something like, "OK, you know when to go," or some other positive word or phrase.

Fantasies

There are a host of fantasies that you can call up while you run. The best are the ones that you make up yourself; here are a few suggestions, however, from Dr. Jerry Lynch's book, *The Total Runner,* and a few suggestions of original design.

- Imagine yourself floating in the front of the lead pack at the New York City Marathon.
- As you run up a tough hill, visualize being suspended by helium balloons or being gently guided and pushed by a giant hand on the small of your back.
- Let your running partner get in front of you, and imagine a rainbow (or something corny like that), connecting your heads together and begin to feel your partner's energy flow through the rainbow into

your partner's energy flow through the rainbow into your body.

- As you run into the wind, imagine you are shaped like a wedge and you cut through the breeze effortlessly.
- Imagine yourself to be an animal, with the animal's grace, style and strength.
- As you run down a steep hill, look out into the distance and feel like a giant bird, floating to your destination.
- Imagine your body to be a well greased, oiled, and highly tuned machine.
- See yourself floating by the cheering crowds who all came to see you set a new world record.
- Imagine yourself a soldier of war, running through enemy territory with vital instructions. Feel yourself running loose, alert, quietly traversing the rough terrain, alert for the enemy. Imagine the cars as tanks; don't let them see you.
- Pretend that you are being filmed by the pace car for a national network during your favorite race.
- Imagine you are your running idol.
- Imagine there is a barrier around you that lets in nothing but positive thoughts. Negative thoughts bounce off the barrier.
- Feel yourself flying across the terrain as an F-16 fighter jet, cruising just a few feet above the ground.
- Imagine you are running to see your lover after having escaped from a prisoner of war camp.

Dealing With Fears

A runner's mental breaking point can be tested when the outcome of the race looks dismal: fears of slowing, not finishing or being passed in the late stages are demoralizing. The brain sends messages to "throw in the towel" with phrases such as "let him go, it's not important," "I can beat him next time" or "it's too far to continue." Whether you are an elite or recreational runner, the fears and anxieties are similar. The first step to help deal with this crisis is to focus on what can be done now. If the grandfather clock knew how many times it had to tick in its lifetime, it would have given up long ago (Lynch, 1987).

By dividing the task into smaller, manageable parts, you can continue, with confidence. As that runner goes by, hang on to him, not until the end of the race but for just "X" amount of minutes or miles. At that segment re-evaluate your feelings. At worst you will have run better for that segment. At best you may catch a second wind and run one of your better races (Lynch, 1987). Or try "reliving the moment" (click back/click up).

Psyching Ploys

There are many ways to psych out an opponent. However, the underlying principle is that you want your opposition to think that you are better than he is. You want him to doubt himself. In the process you will feel more confident in your own abilities. There are dozens of ways to psych out an opponent; below is a partial list:

- Talk to your opponent during the race. He will think you are fresh.
- Wear bright colors. Some believe that staring at day-glo socks is hypnotic and as long as they are staring at your feet, they aren't passing you.
- Sunglasses. Modern sunglasses may make you look faster and more confident to your opponent.
- Name on back of jersey. If they saw you in front of them before, and you beat them, they will remember that name. They will then say to themselves, "I can't beat him; he beat me last time." Nicknames are

especially memorable. My race jersey has GUMBY on the back. People also see your name and cheer you on personally.

- Shaved legs. Shaved skin makes the underlying muscles look more defined. This look may make your competitors think you are better than they.
- Silence. Say nothing. Have a look of seriousness about you. There is something scary about a lack of words. Just don't be rude.
- Look serious. Focus your eyes straight ahead.
- Wet your hair. This will serve to make you look "cool" and keep you cool at the same time.
- Wear black. There is power in the color black. It is dominating, threatening. Just don't wear it on a hot day.
- Clean racing flats. They look sharp and faster than dirty ones.

Some runners like to brag about their supposed personal records at the beginning of a race. Never let them psych you out. Never do this yourself. This only gives someone the opportunity to prove you wrong. Besides nobody likes a conceited racer. Remember that it is advantageous to look like you are here for business, but be friendly. Runners are some of the nicest people in the world; treat them so. You probably have more in common with your opposition than you think.

Pain And How To Manage It

Truly peak performances are often characterized by a complete absence of pain, sound, or thought. Things just sort of happen and you look back and say, "I can't believe I did that." Unfortunately, most races aren't like that. Pain is usually associated with high-level efforts.

It is crucial to associate with pain, to recognize it and

assess it before we try to ignore it. For pain may be an indicator that you are pushing an anaerobic threshold and (depending on where you are in the race) may have only minutes or seconds left at your current pace.

The importance of evaluating your body's pains is to determine whether the pain is a sign of pushing too hard or is simply a nuisance. Identifying with your body's signals will allow you to run as fast as you can, without pushing to the point of collapse. When we begin to feel pain we should undergo a series of steps in dealing with it. Experienced runners may do this automatically or naturally. Less experienced runners may wish to follow these recommendations.

Pre-Pain Association

Pain is something that is often easily diverted from our conscious mind and often we get too swept up in emotions to feel pain. A classic example of this is going out too fast the first mile of a marathon. This excessively fast mile is not difficult enough to channel the pain into our conscious mind, but it is fast enough to cause premature fatigue.

Should you attempt to run the first mile all-out, you can bet you'll feel it. However, going out 30 to 60 seconds too fast is entirely possible without feeling a lick of pain. So the first essential part of associating with your body is to monitor your body's signs of effort, without using pain as an indicator. Your breathing, turnover rate, perceived speed, body heat, stride length and running form are all excellent tools of measurement.

Pain Association

Once our emotions have settled down, pain is more easily identified. Once we feel pain, we should associate with it. Check your body, see how things are going. Does the pain warrant slowing down? Your own experience is the only real indicator of what action needs to be taken. If this pain is a sign that you are going too fast, perhaps you do need to slow down. If not, you'll need to deal with it somehow. To do so you can use one or more of the many techniques that will follow in this section.

After you deal with the pain, and depending on the length of the race, you will need to come back and associate with your body again. You ought to make sure that you are running within limits that will allow you to finish at ideal speed. Perhaps you can check back in with your body every mile mark of a marathon or every lap mark of a 5,000-meter race.

If you can not shake the pain, it does not necessarily mean that you need to slow. Certainly, the pain down the final stretch of a half-mile race can be excruciating, but this does not mean you should decelerate. There are times when all the pain in the world does not mean it is time to slow. You must learn to accept that pain, or ignore it entirely. Once again, some of the strategies of pain management discussed in the next few pages will work.

What To Do When You Feel Pain

P (erception)—Perceive the pain

A (ssociation)—Associate with it. Analyze it.

I (ntervention)—Use a strategy to deal with it.

N (egation)—But now and then check back with it.

We now know that there are many times when it is crucial to examine perceived pain. We know that we must judge our pain as an indicator of how hard we are working. Should we determine that our level of pain does not signify impeding doom, we may choose to use a strategy to eliminate or reduce this pain, so as to prevent it from negatively influencing our mental state. The following techniques are helpful for just that.

Disassociation

Simply getting your mind off the pain is the art of disassociation. Whether you are thinking of your race strategy, form, or thinking about what to cook for dinner tonight, you are disassociating from the pain. You are simply shifting your attention.

The Black Box

This strategy, taken from Jerry Lynch's *The Total Runner*, proves often to be effective in disassociating with pain. During a point in the race when you need to put pain aside, such as the third quarter of the race, or up a hill, you simply imagine pulling the pain out of your body. It looks like a ghost of you as it slowly comes out and brings you relief. Then crumble the pain up into a ball, compact it down, squash it. Take the pain in your right hand and with your left see yourself opening a small, black box. Now take the pain and shove it into the box. Tuck the corners in, and quickly close the lid so that none of the pain is sticking out. Then take a padlock and snap the lock shut. Now toss the box as far away as you can. The pain is now locked up permanently and will not interfere with your race again. Should it somehow creep out, though, lock it up again with a bigger lock.

Employing this strategy at the very minimum works to keep the pain away as long as it takes you to visualize it all. Because of this I recommend taking some time to complete the process. At best a technique like this may eliminate the feelings of pain from your conscious mind entirely.

The Envelope

Another version of the black box is to see yourself writing a letter (disassociation which takes away from the pain in itself) that says something like, "I will deal with the pain when I open the envelope." Address the envelope to "The End of the Race." Now see yourself pulling the pain out of your body, stuffing it into this envelope, closing and sealing it. Now send it away ("mail" it) and deal with it at the end of the race.

Excitement

As previously mentioned, a natural and effective way of relieving our pain is to shift attention away from it. Just like when we have a mild earache all day long and rarely notice it until we lie down in bed and feel it throbbing. Our attention can be diverted away from pain.

The best diversion for the runner is that of excitement. A common reason for personal record races being achieved without feeling a lick of pain is that we grew so excited about the heady pace we were running and at the prospect of breaking our personal record or winning the race, that we simply became preoccupied and never noticed the pain.

This experience happens quite naturally, but can be somewhat artificially induced. How can you purposely excite yourself in a race? Well, first you need to choose *when* to excite yourself, then you simply use visualization. As you race see yourself hammering your finishing kick, leaving the competition in the dust, smashing your personal record, or breaking a world record.

Click Back/Click Up

This is another method for disassociating with pain—a process we have touched upon before. When I teach it in a mental training session I describe it like this. "Think back to a peak race . . . a race when things just unfolded without effort. Remember the sensations of flying along, without effort. You felt as if you could run that pace forever. Now bring those feelings, those sensations to this race."

Your emotional state is a powerful influence over your pain tolerance. By tapping into the memory stores from a previous peak performance we may be able to capitalize on serves as a form of disassociation.

Talk To It

"Well it's you again?" "Don't you get tired of trying to make me slow?" "You know it never works." "Well, it was nice to see you again, but I can't spend much time dealing with you now; I'm in the middle of a race, and, well, I must start running faster now." "See you later."

Blow It away

As the wind passes you, simply imagine the wind blowing the pain off you.

Magic Water

As you pass the water stop take some water, and as you drink it feel it soothe as it runs down into your body, killing the pain and revitalizing muscles. Pour some over your head and let it wash the heat and pain away. The water is like a powerful fuel and consuming it brings about an automatic increase in pace.

Exhale It

Take a deep breath and then exhale all the pain. Visualize the pain flowing out with your breath. This technique will also help you relax, which will bring about faster running.

Run Away From It

Imagine your pain running beside your body, keeping stride with you. Now you decide that you are tired of this nuisance. You pick up the pace to one which your pain shadow cannot hold. See yourself running away from the pain. "Goodbye, my friend; see you at the finish." Now laugh as the pain is itself . . . in pain.

Chapter 4

MOTIVATIONAL TOOLS AND TECHNIQUES

For the Runner and Coach

I. The Measure of Your Miles: The Logbook

If there were a fire in my home the first thing I'd grab would be my running log. This log contains years of my life. Its pages are filled with information about me. I laugh as I read my beginning days, what I thought was fast, what I thought was heart-breaking. I cry at memories of past friendships and dreams that were never realized.

Always in the back of my mind is that while I'm reading the pages of this month's workouts, some day I will look back at this page with the same emotions as I look back to the others now.

As nostalgia, this book is unbeatable. It contains all the times I ran, all the awards I won, all the friends I had, all the pain I endured. Without having kept this daily log, I would have long forgotten old times, races, friends, and who I was. It is a valuable tool for motivation. The log is priceless! And besides, it solves those "remember when" arguments.

Beyond the sheer pleasure of the log's nostalgia, it also serves as a tool to help you become a better runner. By logging your daily workouts, your weekly, monthly, and yearly mileage, you can help determine which form of training pyramid has worked best for you. You can determine what the optimal workouts were for you for a particular distance. You can determine how much tapering worked best. Careful analysis of your logbook throughout the years can serve as the most important technical tool in developing a workout schedule.

By listing under an "other" category, you can keep track of minor pains and delay the possibility of injury through early detection. Without the log we tend to forget the little pain we had a few days ago. Taking note of a "little right knee pain" over a few workouts may tell you to take a few days off now, before you are forced to take a few weeks off later. You may also see what form of training led to the most injuries of your career by analyzing your workouts and injuries.

Keeping a section in the back of your logbook to chart personal record progress proves an interesting venture. Seeing your progress helps to keep you motivated. You can look back and say, "Hey, look at this three-year period without a personal record; I never thought I'd PR again. Then I did, and I will again."

If you race the same course or distance continuously, you may easily determine which strategy works best for you. You may discover that your best 10K times came from racing a particular strategy. Writing down and re-reading the tactics you employed in your race will help you remember them, so you can use them effectively again. You may note how one of your competitors used a particular strategy, or a location on the course where he was particularly weak, and you can hopefully have an advantage the next time you race against him.

You may also determine what mind-set works best for you. Analysis of the last 10 years of my races shows that 90%

of my personal records were achieved when there was little or no pressure on me. In fact, many of my personal records were set when I had no intentions of racing at all; and I "felt good, so kept picking it up." It will also help you determine what diet works best for you. "Threw up after race" will tell you what may not be the best meal to eat before competition.

Keeping track of your mileage on a weekly basis will help you increase your training in small increments, so as to avoid injury. I personally choose, however, not to record weekly mileage since it puts too much pressure on me and sometimes pushes me to overtrain.

Tracking your monthly and yearly mileage provides you with the opportunity to develop some truly personal records. I keep track of all my personal records—not just my fastest times, but "the most miles run in a month," "the most miles run in a year" or "the fastest combined 5K-10K double," and so on.

These personal records provide an additional boost to your sense of self. I am more fond of my 10,000-mile shirt than of my first marathon shirt. I had planned on logging the 10,000th mile during the 25.2-26.2 mile mark of the Los Angeles Marathon. I decided that for the sake of training I was best to log it the week after. I slowly circled the track for that final mile with my entire team. Afterward they all signed the shirt I wore. This kind of memory means more to me than my fastest times.

The logbook also serves as an excellent place to write down your goals. Every time you record your run, you can see the reason you did it; the goal is staring you in the face. Affirmations are valuable when kept in the logbook too. Affirmations of dedication are especially valuable in the log book. Here is a list of 10 reasons to keep a running log.

1. Nostalgia.
2. Keep track of mileage, milestones, and personal records.
3. Determine what form of training works best for you.
4. Determine what mental techniques work best for you.
5. Prevent injuries by using moderation in training.
6. Determine what strategies and tactics work best.
7. Determine what diet works best for you.
8. Write down goals and affirmations or inspirational slogans to yourself..
9. Calculate how many miles your shoes have on them.
10. Settle "remember when" arguments.

To summarize, here are some things you should record in your logbook:
- Details of workouts and races:
  a. Date and time
  b. Type of workout, race, time trial
  c. Mileage or distance
  d. Elapsed time
  e. Location
  f. Other—companions, weather, food eaten and when, etc.
  g. General comments and reflections—"felt good," "had no kick," etc.
- Monthly, yearly mileage
- Personal records
- Inspirational messages to yourself
- Goals—short- and long-term.

It is important to log your runs each evening. That way you will get into the habit and won't forget. I also

Sample Log Page

Date	Type	Miles	Time	Location	Other

recommend logging your races as soon as possible. You may wish to discuss in your logbook other race-related information: name of race, duration of warmup, pre-race strategy, splits, strategy utilized, tactics utilized, competitors and their strategies and weaknesses, shoes worn and the tough part of the race and how you dealt with it.

Do not become a slave to your logbook, however. It can become easy to push yourself when you don't feel like running. You shouldn't run simply because you wanted to do "X" number of miles for the week, or you wanted to run every day. Type-A personalities are especially prone to becoming a log slave. It is far more important to read your body than your log (Miller, 1991).

II. Affirmations

The subconscious mind is the controller of the way we think, act, and perform. And the most effective way to program yourself mentally is through your own self-talk. The things we say to ourself have great impact upon how we think of ourself. "Thoughts about how you will do in a race and how you ought to do have a profound impact on performance. They can set you up for success or set you up for failure" (Elliot, 1984).

Enter affirmations. What is an affirmation? Positive self-talk. Positive, present, self-talk. The affirmation should be positive in two senses of the word. The first is obvious— in that it should have something desirable to say. Obviously, we don't want to develop an affirmation that says, "I'm a lousy runner."

The affirmation should give some direction, some positive concept of what is desired. It would be futile to make an affirmation that said, "I'm not going to go out too fast."

Continue reading for examples of positive affirmations.

I want you to picture in your head a dog *not* chasing a cat. OK, what did you see? Whatever you saw, you didn't see a dog not chasing a cat. Perhaps you saw a dog and a cat sitting. Perhaps you saw a dog playing the cello. What you saw was a positive image of something. For the mind works in positives, not negations. No wonder kids don't remember when their parents say, "Don't play in the street." What the parents need to say is, "Play in the park."

When we tell ourselves "don't" we fail to retain it. If I say to myself, "I am not going to go out too fast," I have given myself no direction as to what to *do;* thus anything could happen. What needs to be said is "I'll go out in 5:10." This gives direction.

Let me give an illustration via a non-running example. Children who were beaten by their parents, when they become adults they may say to themselves, "I'm not going to hit my kids." They sincerely do not wish to hit their kids. However, their statement of "I am not . . . " fails to reprogram their mind-set. What they need to say is, "When my kid acts up I am going to . . ."

When I ask one of my runners what he is going to do in the race, he knows if he says, "I'm not going to get pushed to the back," I will jump on him and say, "I don't want to know what you're *not* going to do, I want to know what you are going *to do.*" "I'm going to stay in the back of the first pack, coach." "Good."

In addition to being positive, an affirmation should be in the present tense. The idea of an affirmation is to program your mind toward success. If I desire to be a 4:15 miler, I would profit from developing an affirmation that programs me into believing that I *am* a 4:15 miler. Thus the affirmation might simply sound something like this. "I am a 4:15 miler." If a high school miler's goal is to win his league, he might say, "I am the fastest runner in the league."

This certainly is not to say that future tense affirmations do not work; they do, but not as well. Remember that some of the best affirmations for you might be the biggest bold-faced lies when you first begin using them. They are stretches for you; they are what you hope or expect to be true in the future. It is important that you say them as if they are already true; the more you say them, the more they will become true (Porter, 1990).

Affirmations are simple. Just decide what you desire and create your own affirmation. Make sure it is positive and present, and I recommend that you keep it short, memorable, and usually begin it with "I". It also helps if an affirmation rhymes.

"Loose and relaxed, I run my max"
"I am the greatest."
"I am the best runner in the league."
"I always perform well under pressure."
"What my mind can conceive and believe I can achieve."
"I love hills"
"Coach believes in me; I believe in me"
"I run smoothly, and I am powerful."
"I am in control of the race."
"I am a master of the mile [marathon or whatever]."
"If it is to be, it is up to me."

So just how can you use affirmations to help you? Ideally you not only use them to achieve your goals, but you can use them to help you with your weaknesses. For example, if you have a difficult time with the hills halfway through your race, you can develop an affirmation(s) to help you with them.

"I utilize hills to my advantage."
"I am the best hill runner in the race."
"I bound up death hill with ease."
"I love hills."

"Hills are my friends."
"Hills are the strongest part of my race."

Once you develop an affirmation, it is beneficial to repeatedly say it aloud to yourself. The little engine had it right when he said, "I think I can, I think I can." In fact, he would have been better to say, "I can" or "I am." Either way, what the little engine knew was that the more an affirmation is repeated—or any message for that matter—the more we will store it, believe it, and be it. Advertisers know this. This is why they repeat messages over and over again.

Repeating an idea six times will change 63% of people's minds. Seventeen times will change 98% of their minds (Moore, 1989). No wonder Coca-Cola and Pepsi continue to bombard us with their slogans. If either gives in, the other will win.

We can make use of this proven technique by repeating our affirmations over and over. I strongly encourage writing your affirmations down and posting them in a place where you will continually read them. Perhaps on your bathroom mirror or the refrigerator door. Say them to yourself daily, they will become true.

I encourage all runners to develop an affirmation that they can use during a race. Personally, I say "Loose and relaxed I run my max" over and over in my head while racing. I have even been known to say my affirmations out loud while racing. I was embarrassed once during a 20 mile time trial where around mile 16 I was exclaiming to myself, "I'm a stud, I'm a stud." I don't know exactly what the passing girl thought. All affirmations, both positive and negative, are likely to become self-fulfilling prophecies (Porter, 1990).

III. Goal Setting

During the final, agonizing miles of a marathon the pain becomes intense, your muscles cry out, your head rationalizes thousands of reasons to quit. What then keeps you going? Your goals. Goals add fuel to the fire of motivation, and give you reason to tolerate the pain.

I recommend that you set and write goals for a variety of aspects. Set them for individual races, seasons, and life. For every basic goal category you create, it is advisable to set three goals. For example, if your current two-mile personal record is 10:30 and you want to considerably improve that during the next season, I recommend you set three goals. Goal #1 should be one that you know is possible to achieve since you have either already done it or came very close to it. Bob Glover in his book, *The Competitive Runner's Training Book*, calls this an acceptable goal. For our 10:30 two miler it may be 10:20. The next goal is one that you know with considerable work, and some luck, you can obtain. For our two-miler this may be 10:10. Finally, you have your dream goal; go for it on this one. Our two-miler may aim for 9:55.

The purpose of setting three goals is to optimize your chances for success. If our 10:30 two-miler had only set one goal of 9:55 and fell short running 10:03, he might be disappointed because he missed his goal. However, by creating three goals he has met two out of three and is successful. Furthermore, setting three goals helps you to obtain that ultimate goal by giving you intermediate steps along the way. There is inherent satisfaction in achieving those first goals. It breaks the stretch up from where you are now to your ultimate goal. Smaller goals will help you to achieve a bigger one.

Once you have formulated your goals, post them in a place where you can see them—preferably alongside your affirmations. Believe in yourself, but set goals that are within reason. It is far better to set goals that are too low than too high, for you can always meet them and then set new ones. Believe in them!

Goal 1: Acceptable goal.

Goal 2: Challenging goal.

Goal 3: Dream goal.

Pre-Race Script

Having the runners write down just how their race will go the day or a couple of days before the race is a valuable exercise. First, it forces the runner to think of how he will run the race, i.e., plan the race. Secondly, the process of writing the script will also enable the runner to visualize the script. Lastly, a written script of how a race will go will be looked upon more objectively than a verbal one. We are used to picking up things and reading them critically. The script should be written, of course, in pencil to allow for revisions. The coach may choose to employ this tool only before big races. This adds some significance to the event. Conversely, if the coach is trying to take pressure off the big race, he may want to use this tool before each and every race.

Post-Race Analysis

So what happened? My mentor/coach used to say, "plan your race and race your plan." This, of course, is sometimes too simple. Nonetheless, a post-race analysis will help the runner determine what he did right and could have done better. The coach may choose to design a form to be copied—like a questionnaire. Or, he may simply say, write a script of how your race went. This helps in the learning process and it's amazing what the coach might learn from the athlete. Sometimes, coach and runner just need to sit down and put what happened on paper. The coach should save the scripts. He might file them and upon the athletes graduation or leaving the program, give them to him—a nostalgic memento.

IV. The Progress Chart

The progress chart allows you to see your seasonal performances logged on a chart. Three lines represent your current performances, goal performances, and the previous season's performances. This chart enables you to see improvement. It also helps break up your three seasonal goals into smaller, manageable increments.

It should be recognized that progress along a direct line to your goals is not going to be, nor should it be, precise and steady. Improvement is always two steps forward, one step back. It is unrealistic to expect to approach your goal on a straight line throughout the duration of the season. The goal line simply serves as a rough indicator of about where you want to be at that point in the season.

The left hand side of the progress chart shows your increments of time. Fill out the times from the slowest you could possibly run to your dream goal. Leave a few spaces above your dream goal, just in case. Simply divide the number of spaces available by how long you want your time span to be and make the increments as small as possible.

Make sure you take into account last season's times as well as this season's predicted times. I recommend using a time column that will allow you to see large drops in time graphically. So for the half-mile design a time line of quarter or tenths of seconds.

The middle of the log has spaces for the names of your races on the angled line, and the date on the horizontal line. You may choose to write in the names of last year's races on the angled lines as well; use a different pen color.

Progress Chart

Name:				Base:					Time Goal 1:				Other Goal 1:			
				Strength:					Time Goal 2:				Other Goal 2:			
Distance:				Speed:					Time Goal 3:				Other Goal 3:			

Race Time																

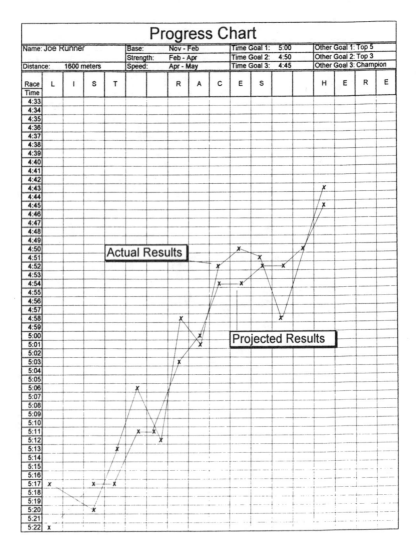

V. Visualization and Relaxation

I cannot stress enough the importance of this type of mental training workout. The benefits to be gained are tremendous. After all, these workouts deal with the most important part of the runner—the mind. Whole books have been written on visualization and on relaxation (I highly recommend them), but I will explain both the process and benefits briefly here.

"The key to smoother, faster running is to concentrate on remaining totally relaxed, rather than putting forth more effort. Relaxing will make muscles more fluid, improve coordination and endurance. Relaxed muscles permit more blood flow and lessen cramping. Relaxed muscles decrease blood lactate and reduce fatigue" (Lynch, 1989).

Recall that every muscle has an opposing muscle. When one of the set is contracting, there is no need for the other to contract, and it should remain relaxed. Excess effort causes a runner to tighten opposing muscles, which delays the primary contraction. Thus, too much effort slows the runner down and contributes to early fatigue.

Tom Osler, an ultramarathon champion describes it like this: "What the distance runner requires is to be able to coast at nearly top speed with unused muscle fibers in a state of complete relaxation while only those necessary to running are working" (Osler, 1978).

Practicing visualization and relaxation techniques teaches the body to run relaxed. Visualization and relaxation techniques also increase the ability to concentrate, to sharpen mental focuses, to endure more pain, to possess enhanced confidence and to help you realize your goals. When the mind is relaxed you can visualize success and reduce fear and panic (Lynch, 1989).

Most runners have set in their minds a pre-conceived

idea of how fast they are capable of running. Usually this limit is considerably short of what their potential actually is. It is important to understand that the mind cannot help to overcome physical limitations; it can, however, help the runner to exceed his self-imposed psychological limits.

Since it is usually our mental state that prohibits us from running our fastest, it makes sense to work on the brain as well as the muscles. An open-minded athlete (Roger Bannister) once challenged the "ultimate barrier" of human endurance, the four-minute mile. His sub-four race was seen as a true milestone. Hundreds since then have gone under the four-minute "barrier." Now a 3:59 mile in a world-class race might put you a straightaway behind the winner.

Every movement we make in life requires a neurological pattern to perform it. The baseball pitcher works years to develop a precise sequence of movements, a neurological pattern that will enable his ball to sail the way he desires it to. As I type now I do not have to think where the letters are that I desire to type, I have a neurological pattern that has been formed by practice and use over the years.

By visualizing ourselves running with perfect form, we are actually enabling the brain to develop a neurological pattern to improve our form. We are teaching ourselves to do so without physical training. Recent studies have also shown that athletes who visualize isometric muscle contractions were shown to have increased gains in strength from that visualization.

A basic study to gauge the effects of visualization (imagery) on athletic performance was conducted at the University of Chicago. Here, young men of equal foul shooting ability were divided into three groups. Group A was told not to practice shooting fouls for the next 30 days. Group B was only to practice foul shots for one hour a day for the next 30 days, and group C was only to *visualize* shooting fouls for the next 30 days.

At the end of the test period the results were as follows: Group A—no improvement, Group B—24% improvement, and Group C—an amazing 23% improvement, without touching a basketball (Wanko, 1992). On the face of things, then, a combination of practice *and* visualization should be even more effective.

The definitive study on the effects of imagery is that of Feltz and Landers (1983). They examined 60 separate visualization experiments and found that 48 supported a correlation between visualization and performance.

Sample Mental Training Session

Here is a possible visualization and relaxation session I might use with my runners.

"Relaxation before a visualization session is important because it creates a receptivity in the mind that enhances the depth of the visualization" (Porter, 1990).

Turn the lights off. "Lie down on your back, hands at your sides; close your eyes."

"Achieve a comfortable position; scratch, stretch or whatever it takes to get comfortable. But no talking, please.

"I want you to concentrate on slowing your breathing down. Pause at the top of each inhalation, and pause at the bottom of each exhalation. Feel your stomach rise as you inhale and fall as you exhale. Slow and deep. Slow and deep. Slow and deep."

I do this until I feel that the runners are calm, serene. Then I move into a more hypnotic mode. "I want you to listen to the sound of my voice and nothing else. Countdown five breaths; with each one you feel heavier and heavier [you may wish to use "lighter and lighter"]. FIVE . . . You are feeling very relaxed. FOUR . . . You feel as if you are sinking into the ground. THREE . . . You are feeling heavier and heavier. TWO . . . You are sinking deeper and deeper into the ground. ONE . . . You are very relaxed now, totally relaxed."

The following allows the runner to achieve total body relaxation. By continually using the key word "relax" a runner will learn to step up to the start line and say to himself: "relax," and his body will be trained to become totally relaxed almost instantly.

"When I say to you GO, you will tighten all the muscles in your legs; and they will raise off the ground about six inches. When I say RELAX you will let them drop. They will be very relaxed and you will not be able to move them. They will be separated from your mind. Ready, Go—1, 2, 3, 4, 5, 6, 7, 8, 9, 10 Relax! You can no longer move your legs, they are separated from your mind."

I then repeat the procedure for the abdominal's and buttocks, the arms and hands, the face and neck. I conclude with all the muscles in the body at once.

The following will build the ability to concentrate. The word "success" is significant in building confidence.

"I want you to picture in your mind the word 'success.' Let no other thought enter your head but the word 'success.' If any other thought should enter your head, simply push it out with the word. Think of nothing but the 'success.'" I let them envision the word for a longer period of time each session. Perhaps 30 seconds is a good place to start.

The next step is to describe a typical race scenario to the runners. Ask them to just imagine that this is happening to them. Start with the warmup, and work through to the warmdown. Include all the preceptor

106

senses, but introduce them one at a time. At the point of the kick, all the senses should be utilized to make it seem real.

"See yourself traveling to the race. You arrive at the meet, step off the bus and take your bag over to where your team usually stretches. See yourself beginning to do a warmup. You are jogging lightly and talking to your teammates. Hear your teammates talking about the upcoming race. You have been jogging for a few minutes now and you begin to break a sweat so you head over to the grass to stretch.

"See yourself stretching, pulling gently on your strong muscles. Hear yourself telling your teammates about how well we are going to race. Feel a little nervousness in your stomach. You have stretched adequately and you hear the first call for your race. You put on your racing flats and proceed to do a few strides. You feel loose and relaxed. See yourself striding along with perfect form, loose and relaxed. You go to the starting line, shake the hands of your opponents and teammates. The gun goes off!

"Take off quickly as to insure a good early position. Your elbows are out to push away anybody who might try to cut in on you. Now you settle into your race pace. You fall in behind another runner. He is breaking the wind for you; he is doing all the work. Feel yourself running totally relaxed. Your fists are relaxed, your shoulders are swinging smoothly and freely, your jaw is loose and open, and your entire body is totally relaxed.

"The runner in front of you is starting to drift away from the pack, so you pull out from behind him, passing him swiftly so that he will not try to stay with you and you pull in behind another runner. Focus on the back of the next runner and work on your relaxation. You come around a corner and hear your coach yelling for you. Hear the crowds cheering for you. See yourself running effortlessly, totally relaxed, confident that you are going to win this race.

"You approach the (whatever lap or mile mark) feeling totally relaxed, totally in control. You begin to feel fatigued, but this will not slow you. You hear the crowds cheering for you and it inspires you to throw in a surge, as you pass the guy you were following. Working hard now you can feel the sweat run down your face. A drop of this sweat runs into your mouth and you can taste the salt.

"You see a hill approaching. You feel confident that you are going to make up ground on this hill. You bound easily up the hill knowing that you will make twice the ground when you surge at the top of the hill. It is a long hill and a grueling one. Feel yourself running up this hill totally relaxed. You are running on your toes with a good forward lean, short strides, pumping the arms.

107

"The crest of the hill approaches and you pick up the pace. The leader is dying at the top of the hill. You focus on his back, feeling totally relaxed, you draw his back closer to you while remaining totally relaxed. Hear your coach yelling for you. You catch up to the leader and pass him quickly. Now you are the leader.

"You approach the (1/3 of the race to go) and you feel confident that you are going to win this race. Although you are fatigued, you are totally relaxed. The runner you passed is closing in on you; hear the pitter-patter of his feet. You pick the pace up a little, but you are tired. Smell the sweat, and feel the heat rising off your body. Hear his foot steps approaching, closer and closer, until he passes you slowly and you drop in behind him and focus on his back.

"Focus right in on the tag on the back of his jersey. Stare at that tag and concentrate on it. Some sweat runs into your right eye, and you feel it sting a little. You hear the roar of the crowds as you sense the finish not far off, but you remain totally relaxed. You feel your self running behind, totally, totally relaxed. Feel your muscles running with perfect form, hear the pattern of your footsteps, hear your breathing, feel the heat rising off your body, totally relaxed.

"The finish line is in sight and you decide that you are going to use a jump kick. You're just waiting for the slightest sign that your opponent is beginning to fatigue. You see it, a subtle skip in his stride. This is the moment. Take off quickly, surprising him. Accelerate past him, driving the arms; hear the crowds cheering for you. Lift the knees; hear your coach yelling for you. Feel the sweat running profusely, feel your muscular legs sprinting with absolute perfect form, feel the heat flowing off your body.

"You can hear your opponent's labored breathing close behind, but you are striving for that finish line, pumping the arms and driving the knees, totally relaxed. The tape draws closer and closer; you smell the hot, dry air and hear the crowd yelling for you. Thirty yards ... totally relaxed, twenty yards ... driving the arms, ten yards ... one last effort and as you hear your opponent very close, you hit the tape! You won!

"You hear the crowd cheering for you and your teammates come over and hug you. You are proud of yourself. You turn around and shake your opponent's hand. You cheer on the rest of your teammates as they sprint in.

"After they are all in, you proceed to do a warmdown. You feel yourself jogging easily, totally relaxed. Feel your muscles running smoothly, with perfect form. Your teammates come over and jog with you. You jog for awhile, then put on your sweats. You are proud of yourself; you worked hard and you deserved to run well."

Often, I will observe sweat appearing on my runners' faces during the visualization session. Runners frequently report to me that they can feel their hearts racing during the visualization. The body actually senses that all this is real. Tricking the body like this allows for the nerves to establish a smooth, relaxed running form, without running!

I now bring them "back to life."

"I want you to forget about running now and listen only to the sound of my voice. With each number you will become a little more awake. FIVE . . . feeling a little more awake. FOUR . . . twitch your hands. THREE . . . wiggle your feet. TWO . . . open your eyes. ONE . . . you are awake."

Sometimes, before I bring them back, I will do more concentration exercises with them. These exercises may also be done while relaxing them before the visualization.

When I bring them back they may be tired and lethargic. Some may have fallen asleep; which is OK.

Turn the lights on and make certain all are awake. Now the coach is provided with the optimum time to talk to his runners. They are tired, thus all ears. I often discuss racing strategy or team problems. After the discussion is over, I tell them to go run and practice what they have learned.

More On Visualization

• I recommend envisioning a particular upcoming race several nights in advance. If the athlete runs the race over in his head many times, then when the actual race is run he will bascially have already done it, and he will just have to act it out.

• When visualizing, athletes report either seeing the pictures from within their own bodies, out of their own eyes, or seeing themselves as an outsider observer. Either way of imaging is fine. Actually, it is important to learn how to do both (Porter, 1990). Seeing yourself from outside will allow you to observe all facets of your form. Seeing from within your own eyes is critical to knowing how you will see the actual experience.

• Remember that it is best always to speak in positives terms. For example, rather than saying, "You don't feel tired," say, "You feel full of energy."

• A session of visualization is ideal the day before the race; however, I do not recommend one the day of a race, for it may make the runner tired.

• I recommend changing race scenarios frequently and always incorporating strategy into the scenarios. If, during the visualization, the coach says, "See yourself taking four quick steps around each corner," the athlete will do so in the race without thinking about it. It will become automatic.

• I often follow a visualization session with a concentration run. (See Chapter 1.)

• When runners become proficient at visualization, I will often add distractions. For example: if I am having the runners visualize the back of another runner, I will pound on the walls, or make some noise to challenge their concentration.

• The coach may decide to do the visualization along with the athletes, which allows him to know just how long to perform each segment, or he may wish to pace back and forth. The trick is to remain a constant. He should not sit quietly for most of the session, and then stand up and walk around. Later, when the runners are proficient in visualizing, he may do so.

• As the athletes become more proficient at the relaxation techniques you will find they can become totally relaxed within moments once they hear the cue word.

• Visualization works for all athletes, in all sports, and is used by most world-class athletes, in one form or another. Shooting foul shots in basketball, double axels in figure skating, getting out of a sand trap in golf—all can be helped by visualization techniques.

VI. Music

Music can serve as an ergogenic aid either in increasing or decreasing your level of arousal. An arousal level that is either too low or too high will hinder your performance (Willams, 1989). Music can help to change your arousal level, depending on what you want, simply by what type of music you choose.

We already discussed self-talk; Brent Rushall, Ph.D., says that there are three types of self-talk that improve performance. The first is task-relevant self-talk ("loose and relaxed, I run my max"). The second type of self-talk is that of mood words or inspirational slogans, such as "I'm a stud" or "Fly!" which have an emotional impact and lead to a physical reaction (Othersen, 1991).

A third type of self-talk can be stimulated by music. The words fall into the category of mood words, yet they are not your own. Singing these words to yourself turns these words into your own. Add to that the power of the music itself and you have an influential motivator. Dr. Rushall suggests using words as in Michael Jackson's *Bad*—"I'm bad, I'm bad, you know I'm bad"—that serve not only as positive self-talk, but are motivational in themselves. That is, if you know that "bad" is positive in this context.

Music and Endorphins

Music has the power to further enhance your running by releasing endorphins from the brain which act as opiates and bind to opiate receptor sites which increases your threshold for pain. These natural pain killers are the same ones that are released when we begin to run. Many believe these pain killers (enkephalin and endorphin) to be the cause of the "runner's high," since not only do these stimulations raise your pain threshold but they arouse nerve centers which are involved in experiencing pleasure (McConnell, 1986).

For these reasons, the use of music may help an athlete's performance. A problem with music may lie in the method employed to hear it during a run. It is disadvantageous to carry a Walkman-type tape player while running. It is too bulky and heavy. The smaller "sports types" are more convenient, since you can slip them into a pocket or press them between the elastic of your shorts and skin. Still, there may be a drawback in that you must choose a station which will inevitably have fast-paced and slow-paced songs—in addition to the commercials. The best method would be to somehow have the music played without your having to carry anything at all.

I occasionally utilize my home stereo and my van's stereo system by placing them on opposite ends of the track and letting my runners do a speed session around the track with the aid of up-beat rock music. This helps them run a better workout, and makes it pass more quickly. I recommend listening to a soft rock station for the warmup and then switching the station to a more up-beat one.

VII. Heart Rate Monitors

Though I have not utilized heart rate monitors in my own training program, Coach Medellin of Esperanza High School assures me they can be a valuable tool. He has his athletes do a variety of workouts with them. For an interval-type workout he has his runners jog slowly until the lower-rate monitor signals and then he has them slowly increase the speed until the upper-rate alarm sounds.

He works with the heart rate monitor right from the beginning of the season. He feels that they are useful to keep an athlete slow when he's doing an LSD workout. For some kids it's the other way around; "they think they are running hard, but with the monitor on they know . . . they are motivated to keep up the effort."

Chapter 5

Counseling and Communication

Roadblocks To Communication
1. ORDERING and COMMANDING—it creates resistance immediately.
2. WARNING and THREATENING—it challenges them to defy you.
3. MORALIZING and PREACHING—instead of saying, "you should, " try saying, "it would be best to . . . " or "my recommendation would be to . . . " or "I would . . ."
4. JUDGING — it sets you too far above them.
5. CRITICIZING — constructive criticism is normally acceptable, when not delivered in front of other team members. Harsh, disparaging criticism, however, is not helpful or effective.
6. FALSE PRAISING — they will know when it is phony.
7. YELLING — when you have to yell, you have lost.

The "I" Message
The "I" message is a communication skill that yields great results. The "I" message is a way of asking, or demanding, in a less threatening manner. It is a way to avoid putting up walls. Perhaps the best way to describe it is through an example.

Instead of saying: "John you're late again," try saying: "John, I have a hard time taking the roll when people are wandering in late."

In the first example John might reply, sarcastically, "Sorrrrryyyy." Or he might have an excuse to pass off. Since the coach's goal is not to hear an excuse but to prevent the behavior from occurring again, the "I" message works better. After the coach says, "I have a hard time taking the roll . . . " the only thing John can really say, is "OK, coach."

Here's another example: Instead of saying, "John, you are too loud," try saying, "John, I need it quiet, please."

In the first instance, you have said the "you" word, which automatically puts his defenses up. Anytime you start telling a person you, you, you, he will defend himself or counter-attack with, "Oh yeah, what about you, you, you?"

Active Listening

Most people don't really know how to listen. The words go in one ear and out the other. When listening to an athlete's problems or concerns, if what is going through your mind is, "What am I going to say when it is my turn to talk?" you are not listening! You are thinking about what you are going to say.

Listening involves looking at the individual, absorbing what he says, and accepting it. That's it. Just listen. The best thing we can often do for other people's problems is simply to be a good ear. Oftentimes an athlete can figure his own problems out simply by unburdening himself to someone.

Active listening utilizes another skill called *mirroring*. Mirroring is repeating back to the runner what he's told you in a concise manner. "So what you're saying is . . . " You're not judging, giving advice or moralizing; you're just listening and rephrasing what was said. By doing this you force the athlete to look at what he has said and to consider it, perhaps from a slightly different angle. And if you reformulate the problem for him another time or two, he may get closer to working out a solution for himself.

When you finally get to the meat of the difficulty you

can ask the athlete what he might do about it, what are his options, and start the process all over again. It is important to recognize that many problems are blown way out of proportion; after mirroring you may get to the root of the problem, opening the door to a reasonable answer.

Praise

By and large, honest, from the heart, praise is a wonderful thing. We like to be praised, children and young adults especially. They yearn for someone they love and/or respect to say, "Hey, you're OK." Praise can come from actions as well as words. A pat on the back, a strong handshake, an approving nod of the head—all are powerful ways of silently giving praise.

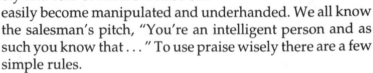

While praise can be encouraging, it can also contribute to anxiety and fear of failure. Praise can easily become manipulated and underhanded. We all know the salesman's pitch, "You're an intelligent person and as such you know that . . . " To use praise wisely there are a few simple rules.

1) Keep praise honest. Don't use praise to soften the criticism. "You ran well but . . . "
2) Avoid using praise to pressure athletes. "You always do so well . . . "
3) Praise is generally not welcomed after a defeat. Praise after a poor performance may well be considered phony or condescending. If the runner knows he had a poor race, telling him he didn't is only putting down his abilities and he will resent it. Simply show support (see Five Stages of Loss, this chapter).

4) Realize that praise may be welcomed but can also be embarrassing, especially in front of other team members who are not being praised. Be careful, praise can be used to unintentionally punish others. If the coach points out five runners and praises them, the others may think, "I guess I'm not good enough for praise." For this reason, praise is often best left to one-on-one situations.
5) Praising the team, however, in front of the team is highly appropriate.
6) Praise is an evolutionary process, you will learn how to utilize it best through a slow process; don't push it.

Cheering And Coaching

"If you lean from your front-row seat in Madison Square Garden and holler, "Looking good!" to Eamonn Coghlan during an indoor mile, you won't be doing him any favors. He wants to be focused; he does not want his concentration broken. But if you and 18,000 other fans let out a collective roar, he can channel that energy in to a peak performance" (Bloom, 1991). Craig Virgin, a three-time Olympian, also considered himself a performer in the hands of the audience. "At Bislett Stadium in Oslo, spectators bang their hands rhythmically on the retaining wall. That really inspires me," he said.

That most runners seem to thrive on souped-up sideline support is undeniable. But what is it that compels runners to expend that extra effort? Why is it some individual encouragements will inspire and others fail? What do you say to a runner in distress?

How spectator support affects competitive performance depends on many factors: who does the cheering, the race distance, how the athlete feels physically, the runner's personality type, and whether or not the runner has a psychological need for such affirmation are all factors (Bloom, 1991).

Of course, highly motivated or competitive runners

may be so driven that they do not need crowd support. In one study, cheering on runners in a treadmill test with standard comments like "looking good" did nothing to change their aerobic capacities or perceived exertion, and actually annoyed them. Further research showed that encouragement tends not to help Type-A personalities but can inspire their more mellow, less self-motivated counterparts (Bloom, 1991).

Coaching should only come from the coach. Friends and parents who attempt to coach generally aren't helpful. I vividly recall one of my team's dual meets. I had given the team the strategy of staying in a group and remaining within striking distance behind the other team's runners for the first half-mile, in an attempt to keep the pace slow. The strategy worked perfectly and everybody was happy except one of the parents who became infuriated with his son who continued to ignore his dad's yelling, "Move up; you've got to be up there; you're too far back."

General support tends to help most runners, most of the time. Saying things like, "Go, Jeremy" or "Come on, Molly," are ideal. These comments simply say, "Hey, I am here to support you and I want you to know I care." That, my friends, is what runners desire to hear. We just want to know that you are there, in our corner. We don't want coaching, 2.23-mile-mark splits, or inaccurate place countings—just support.

Coaches should encourage their athletes to cheer for each other. Phil Ryan at San Marino High School in Southern California has what he calls a "five-minute rule." His athletes have five minutes after they finish their race to jog, get some water, and then begin cheering their own runners on in the next race. The best way to motivate runners to cheer on their fellow runners is to have the team captains and varsity runners set the example.

The Five Stages of Loss

It is important to acknowledge and mourn your losses, have your feelings and accept them. You then go on with life—learning from your experiences, letting go of your defeats, and healing your pain (Porter, 1990).

Sometimes the outcome of a race is not always within your control. Sometimes we simply do not have what it takes physically to do what we desire mentally. How do you let go of a goal after having it for months or years? You must dream, yes, and you must follow your visions. If, after years of hard work, your ultimate dreams have eluded you, you simply let go, acknowledge your achievements, take pride in them, and go on with life. Continue to set new goals and seek out new pathways (Porter, 1990).

Athletes should be encouraged to mourn their major losses. It is important to understand the five stages of loss, to let them happen. Only by experiencing and getting to closure with losses can the runner go on to set new goals, dream new dreams, and live life with vigor and optimism again. These five stages of loss are:

1. Denial
2. Anger
3. Bargaining
4. Depression
5. Acceptance

1. Denial

"I can't believe I lost . . ." "I can't believe this is happening to me . . . " "So many years of training; how could I lose?"

These are a runner's typical initial impressions after a very disappointing loss. Depending on the severity of the loss, this stage can last for days, months, even years for some. Often this stage is marked by the runner acting dazed, almost like he is in a trance.

The denial stage is an important one. Let the athlete experience it . . . put your hand on his shoulder. A commiserating silence is probably better than words.

2. Anger

"I should have . . !" " Why didn't I . . !" "Damn him, he . . !" "Thanks for the great advice, coach!" "Stay away from me; it's your fault . . !"

Anger is the next stage the athlete normally passes through. This stage tends to last longer than the denial stage. I recall watching my top two-miler get pushed off the track during his league finals. As the runner who pushed him made way around the track my runner went through denial in about 200 meters, just waiting there, sitting, in a fog. I knew what was coming next. Anger! I bolted down from the stands, scaled a fence, and made my way over to subdue him just in time to meet stage two. "I'm going to kick his butt!"

When an athlete goes through this stage he may take

his anger out on himself, yelling at himself, calling himself names. Or he may take it out on a competitor or an opposing team. Or, as coaches are well aware, he may rail at the coach.

For this reason, I highly recommend a coach avoid making any comments to a runner until after the runner has emerged from stage two. Wait until he enters stage three before offering counsel or commiseration.

3. Bargaining

"Please, God . . ." "If I could just have another chance, I'll . . ."

These are the words of the bargaining stage of loss. Generally, the bargaining stage does not last long. Minutes at most. Often it is only one sequence. This stage makes way for the painful one. That of depression.

4. Depression

"All I wanted was . . . " "It's not fair . . . " "I have worked so hard . . . " "Why me?"

We are all familiar with the miserable feelings associated with this stage. We have all been there, and we should sympathize and support anybody in such a state. This stage usually lasts the longest.

As I've said, it is sometimes important to mourn a loss. If you are not affected, disappointed, depressed, you may not care enough or have not been involved enough. But it may be important for an athlete to delay his mourning until a better time. For example, it is essential to postpone mourning if you are competing again later in the day. In this case, the coach can help delay the dejection by approaching the athlete and saying,

"Listen (put both hands on his shoulders and make him look at you), it is OK for you to feel this loss, but not now! We still have another race you are needed for. We will worry about what happened in this race later. Go warm up for the next race just like you have done hundreds of times in the past. Think about your strategy; where are you going to make your moves? (Wait for an answer). What pace are you going to take it out in? Be sure you're well warmed up and ready to go. OK? OK? Look me in the eye and say OK. Good, now go over there and run your warmup with the guys. Don't complain or speak of your disappointment; it's not fair to *them*. And Tim, you're all right!"

It is possible that the athlete will do well enough in this next race to actually take much of the pain away. It is also possible that the athlete will bomb again, making things worse. That is athletics, that is the difference between a competitor and a runner. One takes chances. You must get out there and do your best!

When an athlete is in depression, and it is an acceptable time for it, this is normally the right time for the coach to intervene. But don't rob him of his depression by telling him everything's OK. It's not, certainly not for him. Just be there for him and let him know you care.

5. Acceptance

The final stage in the five stages of loss, is that of acceptance. In time, acceptance will come. The depression stage may last for minutes, hours, days, or sometimes months. Eventually, however, the acceptance and recovery stage will come. This stage has been reached when the athlete again looks forward to his next race, season, or goal.

In the best circumstance, the whole thing has been a learning experience, something the athlete can profit from and grow. This growth experience is the reason for athletics, for without it, competing would be an empty risk with little payoff or personal reward.

Chapter 6

The Team Environment

Team Cohesion

A higher level of team cohesion has been of interest to coaches and sport psychologists primarily because of the possibilities that cohesiveness might be linked to superior team performance. There has been a good deal of research on the effects of team cohesion and performance, often with contradictory results, but more studies than not support the idea that there is a positive connection.

Performance variables aside, other benefits of group cohesion include lower absenteeism and dropout rate, and better communication. "Quite simply, the level of communication related to task and social issues increases as the group becomes more cohesive. Group members are more open with one another, they volunteer more, they talk more, and they listen better. In short, the exchange of task information and social pleasantries increases with cohesiveness" (Carron, 1986).

Collective Efficacy

Though there is little research in the field, it is my contention that the more cohesive a team is, the greater its collective efficacy. Collective efficacy is simply the belief in the team's ability as a whole to perform. It is suggested that a team's whole is greater than the sum of its individual parts. A particular runner might, for example, not have much faith in his own abilities but possess great faith in the team. This would be an example of high collective efficacy and low

BOUND-A-ROUND—See p. 21.

individual efficacy.

As with an individual, if a team believes it is powerful, competent, or the best, chances are it will be. A coach can foster collective efficacy by praising the team as a whole, not just the individuals. Stressing the "we" opposed to the "I."

Create A Safe Team

In order to enhance team cohesion (in the hope that performances too will be heightened), it is necessary for the coach to establish and maintain a team environment that is safe and accepting. The runners must feel safety from physical, mental, and social abuse. They must feel like the team is a place that they can come to for acceptance. This secure environment will facilitate better learning and will allow the coach to play all the vital roles he should.

To create a safe team negative traditions must not exist. Hazing freshmen is not acceptable. From the time a new kid steps onto the track he should be welcomed. The coach should be the first one to approach him. A positive first impression is vital. The coach should take a few minutes to explain to the kid what a great team this is and that he is pleased he has come out to join it.

Every new runner should be assigned a big brother/ big sister. The new runner doesn't have to know this. Make the young runner feel special, allow him to participate, and indeed invite him to any social occasions. Make arrangements for him to get to the team's activities.

The coach's personality is the most influential factor as to the safety perceptions of the team. The coach should be relaxed, accepting, warm, and, if possible, humorous. Saying things like, "Well, you're just a freshman," are not helpful or productive.

Conduct Off-The-Track Activities

Off-the-track activities, such as pre-race spaghetti dinners, give the coach the opportunity to talk to his runners in a relaxed, unstructured situation. These occasions give you the opportunity to allow the kids to know you as a person and show them what it is like to be a competent, healthy adult. Allowing them to meet your family, a spaghetti dinner at your home, is even better. This also provides you with the opportunity to know your runners better and will contribute to team cohesion.

Take them to track meets, have ping pong or miniature golf tournaments. Utilize these non-practice situations to see how they are doing in school, in their daily life. Invite them to the coach's office to talk, or simply sit with them on the grass after practice. This is the environment they will remember. These are the times when you can be truly effective in influencing their lives for the better.

Acknowledge Each Runner Each Day

It is difficult to devote attention and personal coaching to each individual on the team each day. Most teams are simply too large. I flatly tell my team, "There are 40 kids on this team, and one of me; if you figure practice lasts two hours a day, that leaves three minutes per individual, if all we did was talk!"

Nonetheless, the coach should make an attempt to at least acknowledge the presence of each runner each day. Whether it be something as simple as a pat on the back, a cheer for him, or actual coaching. When you leave practice that day you should be able to look at your roll sheet and know that you made contact with each individual in some form or another.

Never Embarrass An Athlete

Putting an athlete in a race where he does not belong will be embarrassing. Teenagers especially do not need to be embarrassed. It is better to put them in a race of slower runners where they can be more competitive, or at least competitive with a pack of runners. If you have only the choice of putting them into a race with much faster runners or not racing them, you are probably better off not to run them in that race. Of course, it depends on the athlete, so you may wish to consult him first.

Try The Hart Approach

I was fortunate to hear Gene Blankenship, former coach at Hart High School, speak at a coaching conference. Hart had one of the best cross country programs in the nation for years. Gene gave a speech on how he built the program. Here's an outline.

#1   Bodies—the more you get the more good runners you will get.

#2   Coaching—they had 97 kids and six coaches. Only two of these coaches were paid. Get good local runners to help coach.

#3   Toot your own horn. Don't wait for the cheerleaders to recognize your accomplishments. Develop a bulletin board and newsletter, promote and send results to the local paper, etc.

#4   Recruit kids—from other sports, and watch your kids compete when they participate in another sport. This way you let them know you care.

#5   Develop a consistent team logo, special team colors, etc.

#6   Develop your own special award to be given at the coach's discretion. Hart used pins called Ruby pins.

#7   T-shirts for everything.

#8   Money. It is necessary to do anything. There are a number of ways to raise funds in the community.

The Runners' Court

The Runner's Court is a system that I have developed to handle inter-athlete problems on the team. It stemmed from the following situation: I had a positive and highly cohesive group of runners one year until I got a new batch of freshman. The freshmen were particularly immature. For the first time in my coaching career I had runners actually hitting each other.

The problem was that the runners were so immature (and never wrong) that they would not listen to anybody. My punitive measures at first were attempts at constructive discipline. I had the freshmen wash the seniors' cars or something like that. The cohesion amongst the freshmen crew did not improve. I kicked a few off the team, chased a few away, and still had freshmen fighting.

Desperate for a solution I decided to try what I call the Runner's Court. I didn't really think the runners would go for it, but they rather liked the system. It works just like a regular courtroom. I have the team's seniors (six runners is best) sit on the bottom row of the bleachers, and they act as the jury. I have the two in dispute sit a few rows up and face the seniors. I am behind the seniors and the rest of the team sits behind the "defendants."

The layout is specific so that the defendants talk to the seniors and cannot see the rest of the team behind them. This is done so that the coach may ask questions of the rest of the team without the defendants seeing who is raising their hands to answer the coach's questions. For example, if one of the runners says, "I didn't hit him," the coach can say, "Any of you see him hit him—please raise your hand." The defendants, with their backs to the team, cannot see who responded. The coach stands at the bottom and acts as lawyer for both sides in the dispute.

The seniors hear both points of view and deliberate to determine who, if anyone, is at fault. The coach does not decide guilt or innocence. The seniors and coach then decide on a punishment, if necessary. The coach then announces the punishment and an explanation of why that punishment was decided upon.

You may be wondering why this system seems to work so well:

1. It makes all the runners a part of solving the team's problems.
2. All the runners know what happened, who did what, who said what. They all heard the arguments and likely will have agreed with the seniors' verdict. This prevents runners from going up to teammates and saying, "So and so did this to me and can you believe coach is punishing me?"
3. It empowers the seniors.
4. Nobody is made out to be the bad guy except for the person who was actually the troublemaker.
5. After the case, the matter is closed. The team goes back to doing what it is supposed to be doing.

The whole process does not take very long. If a senior is one of those implicated in the problem then you are probably wise to have a jury of the rest of the seniors and maybe another coach or adult. It is not a good idea to have the younger runners come to a verdict on an older one. This may make problems for the younger runners later. Lastly, if anyone does not want to be on the jury, he should have the right not to.

Hire A Coach Blue

Coach Blue is the name I have given to one of my most valuable assistant coaches. Coach Blue answers more questions for me, solves more problems, and inspires more runners than almost any other coach. Coach Blue is perhaps the most unique coach I have ever run into. Coach Blue is not human.

I developed the Coach Blue concept one track season in which I had 43 distance runners, of both sexes, all abilities, and I was trying to train them for the 800, 1600, and 3200. I was, needless to say, quite pressed for time at practice. On a run one day I took my top runners to the side and we discussed what we could do so that I could free up some busy-work time so that I could spend more time coaching. The following is the result.

Coach Blue is nothing more than a blue three-ring binder. This binder is brought to practice daily by me and is actually property of the team. Team members are instructed to use it. It sits on the grass during track workouts and is with me during class lectures, during stretching, and at spaghetti dinners. In the binder there are four sections:
1. Results
2. Motivational Miscellany
3. Training
4. Records

Under the **Results** section I keep all the result sheets from the season. I also keep their progress charts in this section. Coach Joe Kelly of Peninsula High School suggests keeping a profile on each runner with all his races for his four years.

This section can save the coach from having to answer to each athlete what his time was from the previous meet (or any other). It also gives the athletes a place to keep their progress charts without losing them. I go through and fill out their progress charts after each and every race.

The **Motivational Miscellany** section is much like a scrap book. Everything is kept in those plastic protectors that are made to go in three-ring binders and accept a standard size paper. They sell them by packs of 25 in stationery stores. Anyhow, I put in them newspaper clippings, photographs of the team, articles from magazines, our newsletters, poetry from myself or the runners, inspirational quotes, autographs of world-class runners, varsity lettering procedures, cartoons, and so on.

This section is the one the runners turn to the most. I strategically stock things within the motivational section so that they are seen. For example, the runners like to look at the photographs most, so between each page of photographs I will put something educational or motivational, like a quote. This way they see the material I want them to see.

The next section is the **Training** section. You can also call it the team or coach's section. This section contains the workout schedules, for months or days ahead of time. It contains telephone lists, training group information, flyers on upcoming road races, a copy of a training pyramid, a sheet with all the runners' birthdays listed, time equivalency charts, etc.

The last section of Coach Blue is dedicated to **Records.** In my Coach Blue, I keep yearly records, school records, state, national and world records. *Track & Field News* magazine is the source for such information. The March 1996 issue, for instance, contained the latest world, American, collegiate, junior college and high school records, plus all-time world and U.S. best-performer lists. I also have created a list of unique school records such as most 5-minute milers in a season, all-time lists, etc.

Discuss Race Strategy

A race strategy serves more than the purpose of motivating the athlete, it also empowers him. Having both an individual and a team plan gives the athlete a direction to follow. It is usually best if the strategy is developed together. I personally make sure that each runner has a specific strategy going into each big meet. I often don't worry about it in smaller or less important meets.

Post-Race Analysis

Coach Randi Rossi of Irvine High School in Southern California has each of his athletes write a post-race analysis of his race. Randi then reads each of their written evaluations and makes comments on them. I would recommend the athletes keep these evaluations in their logbooks or scrapbooks, as they might provide some insight to the athlete. It would also be wise for the coach to photocopy and re-examine the analyses at his leisure, as he might gain more knowledge about his athletes' thought processes.

Mileage Clubs

Many coaches employ this technique to help keep the athlete motivated during the summer. A possible summer goal, for instance, is to reach 500 miles. If they do so, they become members of the 500 Club. Giving a T-shirt for the accomplishment will serve as an extra motivator, as will recording their names in your Coach Blue and on the bulletin board.

Workout Schedules

A tentative workout schedule for the month can help motivate the runners in that they understand better what's in store. It makes today's workout seem more important, as they can see the logic of the workout and what it is leading up to. It will also keep them looking to the future for the away trips.

Larry Arason, Athletic Director at Santa Ana Valley High School in Southern California and a cross country coach for 19 years, favors giving the runners a workout schedule at the beginning of the summer for the entire summer. The runners are to put a happy face on the calendar for each day of practice they complete. Larry says, "There'd better be a lot of happy faces at the end of summer."

Newsletters

Though the coach can develop a newsletter, I believe it best for the runners to do it themselves. The team should pick a name for the newsletter and then print one every month or so. The coach can submit articles, but most of the material should come from the athletes themselves.

The newsletter should always be positive and motivational. The coach should review it before it is run off. It can be distributed to the runners, the parents, teachers, administrators, team prospects and posted on the bulletin board.

There are many things you can include in the newsletter. Coach Rossi from Irvine High School includes results, previous course bests, scores, a key for next week, goals for next week, athlete of the meet, and current articles from magazines.

I also recommend including photographs, poetry, tidbits from the past, and team members accomplishments outside the sport. Any way you can give athletes credit for achievements or just being good people is helpful.

Beginning Runners' Packets

I recommend that the coach and team put together a packet for all new runners and their parents. The packet is to explain the workings of the team, who the coaches are, how cross country is run and scored, the meet schedule, the invitationals, the lettering procedures, and anything else pertinent to the team.

I also find this an excellent place to write about the role of the coach and the distinction between coach and parent. You may even have the parents sign and return the last page of the packet to signify that they have read it.

The packet should extol the team's positive points. In my packet I discuss how the team is open, supportive and positive. I clearly state the there are no negative or degrading traditions on the team (freshmen are horridly afraid of being trash-canned). The packet also saves the coach time in trying to explain to the parents why—even though we only scored 15 points—we beat the other team.

Car Washes

Although the primary reason for these is that of fund raising, car washes turn out to be fun events for the team. I recommend making them short in duration (like four hours) and make each member of the team responsible for selling "X" amount of tickets beforehand. The athletes should know where the money is going and have a voice in deciding this.

Yearbooks

Along the same lines as developing a team newsletter is the concept of developing a seasonal yearbook. My team develops one upon the completion of each season. It is geared toward the distance runner and is full of great ideas:
1. Results
2. Articles about the team and its runners
3. Biographies of the coaches

4. Letters of farewell to the seniors
5. Nicknames of the runners
6. Remember when (funny occurrences)
7. Top Ten favorite coach sayings
8. Letters from the graduating seniors to the team
9. Biography of each graduating senior.
10. Photographs
11. Cartoon drawings of funny occurrences on the team.
12. Things that perhaps only the runners understand

Bulletin Board

A bulletin board is the place to display positive things about your team. A primary purpose of the bulletin board is to help recruit other runners for the team. Runners, of course, do like to see their photos, and articles or results, where everybody can see it. I recommend putting a runner in charge of continually updating the bulletin board. Many of the motivational ideas discussed in this book can be posted for all to see.

Mileage Thermometer

Jim Maynard of Marina High School in Southern California has come up with the idea of a mileage thermometer. A large drawing of a thermometer is created and each week the kids move up the thermometer. Perhaps you can put the kids' names on labels fastened to the end of a pushpin. The coach could display the thermometer on the bulletin board for visibility.

Photographs

I often run around the meets taking black-and-white photos of my athletes in action. I then give the negatives to a kid who is in the photo class at school and have him develop them. I then pick a few to make 8x10s of.

You can put them in your Coach Blue, stick them on the bulletin board, or give them to runners as gifts.

Combined Team Dinners And Competitions

To help foster harmony between teams, I occasionally invite one of our competing teams to join us for dinner. The emphasis is on getting to know each other and having a fun time. I find this helps the teams understand each other and appreciate their competition. It is hard to be prejudiced toward another team when you know the members individually.

All my experiences with this have been positive. I often try to have some fun form of competition between the teams that is non-running related—ping pong or something. If the athletes see the coaches conversing and having a good time, so will they. I recommend wearing name tags to help break the ice.

Develop An Alumni Race

The development of an alumni race serves the purpose of letting the kids see that running can be a lifelong sport. There is a 4th of July race that begins in front of our school in Huntington Beach every year. Though it is not just an alumni race, it is great for me to be doing a warmup with my team and to have former runners constantly coming over to talk. I tell my kids that all my runners eventually come back to running (if they ever quit) and this serves as the proof.

Phil Ryan at San Marino High School started an alumni race for his team, and it has expanded to include other teams in the area. He says that it has turned into quite an event, with runners flying back from college to take on the other teams.

Dinner Bets

In Coach Blue I have posted requirements for winning a free dinner from me. I have set the standards at things like beating one of my high school personal records, all-time personal records, breaking a school record, or whatever.

To make it a little fairer I have also established guidelines for when my runners must buy me dinner. They must buy me dinner when they win a league, county, or other championship, receive a scholarship, etc. I recommend that guidelines be set on just what constitutes "dinner."

End Of The Season Survey

At the close of each season it is well worthwhile to develop and distribute a questionnaire to the team. Ask the students to answer honestly and anonymously.

1. What are my coaching strengths?
2. What are my coaching weaknesses?
3. How could I improve?
4. What do you think of the team environment?
5. What else could the coach do for the team's sake?
6. What do you think of the coach's personality?
7. What do you think of the disciplinary measures?

I recommend that you read the survey and evaluate it. Throw out any results that are blatantly frivolous and take the others into consideration. It would then be a fine idea to tell the team that you have read the surveys, and you are going to work on . . . Try not to take criticisms personally. It is wise to keep and file your survey results. Over time you will notice how you have changed, and how it has affected your team.

Bibliography And Suggested Readings

Bloom, Marc. The roar of the crowd, *Runner's World,* April 1991.

Cavanagh, Peter (1990). *Biomechanics of Distance Running.* Human Kinetics Publishers, Champaign IL, p. 190-293.

Carron, A.V. (1980). *Social Psychology Of Sport.* Movement Publications, Ithaca, New York.

Carron, A.V., & Chelladurai, P. (1981). The dynamics of group cohesion in sport, *Journal Of Sport Psychology.* 3, 123-139.

Carron, A.V. (1982). Cohesiveness in sport groups: Interpretations and considerations, *Journal Of Sport Psychology,* 4, 123-138.

Carron, A.V. (1986). The sport team as an effective group. In *Applied Sport Psychology,* Willams, J.M. (ed.). Mayfield Publishing, Mountain View, CA.

Carron, A.V. (1988). *Group Dynamics In Sport.* Spodym, London, Ontario.

Carron, A.V., Widmeyer, W.N., & Brawley, L.R. (1988). Group cohesion and individual adherence to physical activity, *Journal Of Sport And Exercise Psychology.* 10, 127-138.

Cox, R. H. (1985). *Sport Psychology: Concepts And Applications.* Wm. C. Brown Publishers, Dubuque, IA.

Costill, David (1986). *Inside Running: Basics Of Sport Physiology.* Benchmark Press, Indianapolis, p. 35-36.

Edell, Dean, KFI Talk Radio, AM 640, Los Angeles CA, 7/17/91.

Elliot, Richard (1991). *The Competetive Edge: Mental Preparation For Distance Running*. Tafnews Press, Mountain View, CA, p. 118-124.

Feltz, D.L. and Landers, D.M. (1983). The effects of mental practice on motor skill learning and performance: a meta-analysis, *Journal Of Sport Psychology*, 5, 25-57.

Glover, Bob and Schuder, Pete (1983). *The Competitive Runner's Handbook*, Penguin Books.

Lynch, Jerry (1987). *The Total Runner*. Prentice Hall, Englewood Cliffs, NJ, p. 178.

Lynch, Jerry. Relax to the max, *Runner's World*, March 1989.

Miller, Linda. A-okay?, *Runner's World*, June 1991.

Osler, Tom (1978). *Serious Runners Handbook*. Anderson World Publishing, Mountain View, CA, p. 49.

Othersen, Megan. Running dialogue, *Runner's World*, August 1991.

Porter, Kay (1990). *Visual Athletics*. Wm. C. Brown Publishers, Dubuque, IA., p. 5-14 & 141.

Wanko, Micheal. Visualization to enhance training, *SKI Magazine*, March/April, 1992.

About The Author

Eric Anderson is a competitive distance runner, distance coach and student of the sport. He has coached at Huntington Beach High School and Saddleback Community College in Southern California. Anderson graduated from California State University Long Beach with a Bachelor of Science degree in Health Education and received a Masters of Arts degree in Sport Psychology. He is also the author of *The Runner's Doctrine*, a comprehensive text for coaching distance runners. In addition to his coaching, writing and research activities, Anderson has found time to log personal bests of 4:22 for the mile, 31:50 10km, 1:11 for the half-marathon, and 2:44 for the marathon.